By the Word of Their

Testimony

"And they overcame him because of the
blood of the Lamb and because of the
word of their testimony…"
Revelation 12:11

No Weapon Formed Against You will Prosper

NarrowRoad Publishing House

By the Word of Their Testimony
No Weapon Formed Against You will Prosper

Published by:
NarrowRoad Publishing House
POB 830
Ozark, MO 65721 U.S.A.

The materials from Restore Ministries were written for the sole purpose of encouraging women. For more information, please take a moment to visit us at: **EncouragingWomen.org** or **RestsoreMinistries.net**.

Unless otherwise indicated, most Scripture verses are taken from the *New American Standard Bible* (NASB). Scripture quotations marked KJV are taken from the *King James Version* of the Bible, and Scripture quotations marked NIV are taken from the *New International Version*. Our ministry is not partial to any particular version of the Bible but **loves** them all so that we are able to help every woman in any denomination who needs encouragement and who has a desire to gain greater intimacy with her Savior.

Library of Congress Control number: 2015912410

ISBN: 1-931800-29-4
ISBN 13: 978-1-931800-29-7

Contents

Introduction

Your Divine Appointment

*"I was **crying** to the LORD with my voice,*
*And He **answered me** from His holy mountain"*
— Psalm 3:4.

Have you been searching for marriage help? It's not by chance, nor is it by coincidence, that you are reading this book. God has heard your cry for help in your marriage dilemma. He predestined this DIVINE APPOINTMENT to give you the hope that you so desperately need right now!

If you have been told that your marriage is hopeless or that without your spouse's help your marriage cannot be restored, then this is the book you need. Read this over and over so you will begin to believe that God is MORE than able to restore ANY marriage, including YOURS!

We know and understand what you are going through since WE, and MANY others who have come to our ministry for help, have a restored marriage and family! No matter what others have told you, your marriage is NOT hopeless!! We KNOW, after twenty five years of ministry, that God is able to restore ANY marriage, even YOURS!

If you have been crying out to God for more help, someone who understands, then join our Internet Restoration Fellowship OnLine and you'll receive an ePartner (email partner) who will help you see your marriage through to restoration during your rebuilding phase of your jouney. Since beginning this fellowship, we have seen more marriages restored on a regular basis than we ever thought possible!

So, if you are really serious in your desire to restore your marriage, then our fellowship is the answer. For more information or to join, go to our website RMIEW.com. We would love for you to be a part of our Restoration Fellowship!

Who are we and what are we hoping to do?

Restore Ministries helps those who have found themselves in a hopeless situation: couples whose spouse is in adultery, has left, has filed for divorce, or any other seemingly impossible marital situation. These broken people have often sought help, but everyone (many times even their pastors) have told them their marriage was hopeless. However, we not only believe that no marriage is hopeless – regardless of the circumstances—we know they aren't. That's why we offer hope, help and encouragement through our website, our Restoration Fellowship, and a variety of resources including a variety of newsletters to spiritual feed and uplift you daily!

In 2001, Restoration Fellowship was birthed to minister more effectively to the needs of those seriously seeking restoration. Within a year the fellowship grew to over 400 committed members and increases daily with members from all over the world.

Restore Ministries has never sought advertising or paid for placement in search engines but has instead grown by word of mouth. We also take no support from anyone but the individuals themselves who are seeking restoration so that we are never told we must comprise sharing His full truths. Though often ostracized by the established church, because of those who have cried out to God for help when their own church, pastor, family and friends who offered them **no** hope or support, we have given them hope and we have become an oasis in the desert for the desperate, the hurting, the rejected.

Often accused of being extreme, radical, out-of-balance or legalistic, the message in all our resources is founded firmly on the Word of God only, encouraging those seeking restoration to live the message that Jesus proclaimed, beginning with the familiar Beatitudes.

RMI teaches the good news of God's Word to bring healing to the brokenhearted, comfort to those in pain, and freedom to prisoners of despondency and sin through the truth of His Word, giving them the hope that is "against all hope" through the Power of Jesus Christ, the Mighty Counselor and Good Shepherd.

Our site and our resources minister to the hurting all over the world with the intent of creating a deeper and more intimate walk with the

Lord that results in the hurting healed, the bound freed, the naked clothed, the lost saved and broken marriages restored. We minister to women from more than 15 countries including Switzerland, Hong Kong, New Zealand, Sweden, Philippines, Brazil and Germany, with large followings in Australia, Canada, and Africa. Our books have been translated into Spanish, Portuguese, Tagalog (Filipino), Afrikaans, and French. Also Slovakian, Chinese, Russian, Italian and some Hindi.

Jesus said that you "will know them by their fruits" that's why this book and all our *By the Word of Their Testimony* books are filled with testimonies of hopeless marriages that were restored, marriages that give glory to God and to the Power of His Word. Our *WOTT* books are growing at such a phenomenal rate that we were once unable to keep up with getting them published. Now we have a full team devoted to keeping up.

If you have any doubt about the validly of our ministry, you won't after reading this and our other awesome books. Each will show you not only hopeless marriages that were restored, but more importantly, it will show you men and women who have been completely transformed into God-lovers and are now committed on-fire Christians, many of whom were saved through this ministry.

Below is a small sampling of the letters of gratitude that Restore Ministries has received. Please note when you read the letters that they give all the praise and glory to the Lord. This ministry was founded and continues to grow on the premise that "if He be lifted up, He will draw all men to Himself" and "the Lord will share His glory with no man."

"Let Another Praise You" Proverbs 27:2

I am so thankful for the goodness of our Lord and touching my life. Finding this ministry and all they have to offer changed my life, and I give the honor and glory to God for working in me through all the scriptures and testimonies. I can say that God has changed me so much, I have learned so much and I thank the Lord for opening my eyes to the truth. Thank you Jesus for you amazing grace and mercy that you pour our on me everyday and for allowing me to be a blessing to other as well. I don't have words of gratitude and for the joy I have experience through this journey. I have had very hard moments as well, but God has been always been with me and He has always turn all bad things to good. Thank you for the amazing gift of your ministry that changed my life!

I'd like to also recommend "How God can and Will Restore Your Marriage" to everyone! It's a life changing experience and eye opening that led to all the testimonies that you read, Thank you Lord!

When I first found your ministry I was very proud, contentious, bitter, rebellious, selfish, etc. I thought this whole situation with my marriage was my husband's fault and that I had nothing to be blamed about. I was so wrong! Thank you God for opening my eyes! Thank you God for your mercy and grace! I understand now that God wanted me to have a relationship with Him, even though I was a Christian I and I "thought" I had I relationship with God, I did not. Now I can see why. I was ignorant of His word and I thought I had nothing that needed to change, I thought I changed it all. Well, I was wrong! I thank God for showing me the way that lead to life and the way to see my marriage restored. I now don't see my husbands sins anymore but only mine; it's funny how my situation turned around. God also showed me all the things I was doing wrong, and I thank Him for that.

Thank you Lord Jesus for leading to find this ministry! thank you Lord for taking me through this journey and set me free with your truth! I praise you everyday of my life and my lips will sign praises to you forever. Thank you for showing me all my sins and for opening my eyes and allow me to come to a repentance. I praise you all the days of my life for leading me to your word and this course that has changed my life! I cannot thank You enough!

~ Daniela in Arizona

To all the partners of RMI who played a role in providing me with the opportunity to take your courses and read your free books online, thank you very much! I was a one of the lowest points in my life, devastated when God lead me here. It was here that I learn who the real me had become over the years and with a broken spirit I have allowed God to change that person to someone new. I can't begin to express my gratitude to you all. I found my first love, I found God, the lover of my soul. I love my earthly husband but now I love Jesus more. You all have given me more than silver and gold. It's hard to believe as a Christian I've lived my life without a relationship with the Lord; I am ashamed of myself. No one will ever take God's place again. Thanks again.

My first words would be not to say another word to your spouse, nothing, no matter what he or she is saying. I would ask if you wanted your marriage to be saved, I would also say that divorce and separation are never the answers, under no circumstance. I would explain to everyone the reason for both. Yes, I would recommend this site to her.

When I first came here my husband had just moved out. We had tension over several months. What I didn't know was there was an OW, so when I found out I reacted badly, then within weeks divorced paper were filed and that was the end of our marriage without any more talking between us.

Heavenly Father,

Thank You for being so good to me. I was at one of the lowest points of my life and You heard my cry. When I thought You were not listening You were and led me here. You were always with me. I didn't think of restoration, but You did. I had no idea about restoration. Even though I knew in my heart You gave my restoration, I still acted like a crazy woman. I acted within my own useless power and I have no power to change anything. I don't believe I would be divorced if I had stop and listen to you. Thank You for not giving up on me now. Even now You still speak restoration to me. Thank You.

I would like you to know that God can and will restore your marriage. Marriage is God's idea not man so He wants to see you and your spouse married for a lifetime. Your journey begins today, expect more than a restored marriage, expect a relationship that matters even more, a relationship with the Lord that most. If you embrace this truth then your restoration is next.

~ Juanita in Texas

We put this book and all our *Word of Their Testimony* books together because we believe that as you spend some time reading these incredible and awesome testimonies of seemingly hopeless marriages that were miraculously restored, you will be encouraged and know without a doubt...

NOTHING IS IMPOSSIBLE WITH GOD!!

————————————Chapter 1————————————

Nothing is Impossible
with God!

"Looking at them, Jesus said,
'With people it is impossible,
but not with God;
for all things are possible with God.'"
—Mark 10:27

*"And they overcame him because of the blood of the Lamb and because of the **word of THEIR testimony**, and they did not love their life even to death." Rev. 12:11.*

The following testimonies are filled with miracles of men and women who took God at His Word and believed that "nothing was impossible with God!" Those who have had the miracle of a restored marriage have several things in common. All "delighted themselves in the Lord" and He gave them "the desires of their heart." All of them "hoped against hope" when their situation seemed hopeless.

All of them "fought the good fight" and "finished their course." All of them were determined "not to be overcome with evil" but instead to "overcome evil with good." All were willing to "bless their enemies" and to pray for them that "despitefully used and persecuted them." All "turned the other cheek" and "walked the extra mile." All realized that it was "God who removed lover and friend far from" them and it was God who "made them a loathing" to their spouse. All of them understood and believed that it is NOT the will of man (or woman) but the "will of God" who can "turn the heart" whichever way He chooses.

All refused to fight in "the flesh" but chose to battle "in the spirit." None were concerned to protect themselves, but trusted themselves "to Him who judges righteously." All of their trust was "in the Lord" because their trust was "the Lord." All released their attorneys (if that was part of their testing) since they "would rather be wronged or defrauded." All of them "got out of the way of wickedness" and "let the unbeliever leave" since they "were called to peace." All refused to do "evil for evil or insult for insult." All loved their spouse who may have been unfaithful because they knew that "love never fails."

This is the same journey that the Lord took me on back in 1989. That year I made a promise to God that if He would restore my marriage to my husband, I would devote my life to telling others about Him and His desire and ability to restore ANY marriage no matter what the circumstances. The Lord was faithful and restored my marriage, suddenly, two years later after a divorce. (Yes! AFTER a divorce!) Now I faithfully, with the Lord's continued help, love, support, and guidance, spread the GOOD news that nothing—NOT A THING—is impossible with God!

It is important to know that our ministry was FOUNDED to help all those who were told by pastors and Christian friends that their situations were HOPELESS. Those who come to us for hope are facing a spouse who is deep in adultery, who has moved out (often in with the other man or woman they commited adultery with), who has already filed for divorce or whose divorce has gone through. 99% of those who come, come *alone* for help since their spouse is not interested in saving their marriage, but is desperately trying to get out. Over 95% claim that they are Christians and most are married to Christians. Over half are in some type of Christian service and many of the men who are involved with other woman are pastors who have left not only their wife and children, but their church as well.

If you, or if someone you know, is facing devastation in their marriage, there is hope. Read these awesome testimonies that prove that God is MORE than able to restore ANY marriage!

Chapter 2

It Was Me

"Speak kindly . . .
her warfare has ended,
her iniquity has been removed,
she has received of the LORD'S hand
DOUBLE for all her sins."
—Isaiah 40:2

Let me begin by explaining that I was the one who was in adultery. My worldly ways, selfishness, pride and greed made me believe that my marriage should be a certain way. I was hugely influenced by the world, what I read and watch. And I believed we had "issues" in our marriage because it was not how I "thought" it should be. So I filled that void and emptiness in my life and marriage with material and worthless things I thought would make me happy. And when it was not enough, I deluded myself to thinking that friendship with a man is just that, friendship and nothing more. I justified my actions— thinking I was not doing anything wrong. Thinking it could not happen to me, that I knew better. But it was all pride. It CAN happen to anyone. "Therefore let anyone who thinks he stands [who feels sure that he has a steadfast mind and is standing firm], take heed lest he fall [into sin]. 1 Corinthians 10:12

It wasn't until I began my RJ and I learned in my lessons that *we* didn't really have any "issues." It was just me who didn't know how to be the godly wife He created me to be. I was contentious, stubborn and childish. I didn't listen to my earthly husband, wanting to get my way most of the time, if not always. I thought it was okay to challenge him, thinking it's only fair for my "voice" to be heard. I wanted a perfect marriage but I was not willing to change! My pride thought I was not the one who needed changing when in truth, I had a lot of growing up to do.

So I was the one who foolishly brought up divorce thinking the grass is greener on the other side. I was so selfish; everything I did was to have some semblance of control because my life and marriage was falling apart. That's when I made the decision to quit my job and move in with my sister. When I realized all my foolishness, I begged and begged my earthly husband to take me back, to give us another chance again. But my earthly husband, who has always loved me and has been there for me *through everything,* didn't want to be with me anymore. So I had to leave our home for good.

All this time, I turned to family and friends for comfort and help. When I moved in with my sister, and searched the Internet for marriage help. I bought books to read on how to save my marriage. I even bought a psychology packet online that guaranteed to restore my marriage if I did what it said!! I was desperate. It never occur to me to ask the Lord for help.

Even though, I grew up going to church, I didn't really know Him, who He really is. And when I got married, I forgot the Lord in my life completely, thinking I didn't need Him. So when my marriage fell, I sought and was given different advices: worldly and some pointing me to the Lord. But I didn't know what to do, how to approach or open up to Him.

I shared in my BIO that I first found the stander's ministry where I learned that restoration is possible. For a time, I followed what they taught and I learned what scriptures to pray to get him back. But this wasn't enough... I wanted more, but I didn't know what. I didn't know that what was missing was my personal relationship with the Lord. It wasn't enough to recite scriptures, instead, I was longing for that intimacy of knowing whom I was praying to, to really know Him and for Him to know me.

The Lord in His mercy led me to RYM. And *How God can and will Restore your Marriage* book really opened my eyes to understanding my situation, the ungodly wife I was and who I could be in Him. It gave me hope. Real concrete hope. And it said no matter your situation. Even if I was the one who was in adultery.

Though I didn't know what was going to happen or how the Lord would do the impossible, for the first time, I felt different! And I was ready to see where this truth would lead me! :)

Let me also explain that due to my adultery, I had so much guilt with me when I started my RJ. And with guilt, came fear. Fear of the what-ifs, fear of what I couldn't control. Even though I told my earthly husband about the OM, I have not yet confessed that we had been intimate. I was afraid that if I confess, there was no way we would ever be restored. So for a time, I let my ears be tickled, thinking it's enough that I confessed to the Lord.

Yet, going through RMI's online courses helped me to get to know the Lord and His Truths. That He is a loving Husband whose love never changes no matter what you did, have done or will do and Who wants the best for you. So the more I sought Him, the more He strengthened my faith and trust in Him, giving me the strength to confess everything to my earthly husband. I will always remember the verse that convicted me: "He who conceals his transgressions will not prosper, But he who confesses and forsakes them will find compassion." Proverb 28:13. It was one of the most important times I learned about letting go and trusting the Lord for the outcome, whatever it may be. And His Word is true. Instead of what I'd feared, I found compassion when I least expected it!! I found forgiveness. I was finally free, no longer carrying the guilt with me. Free to pursue Him even more and apply His truths in my life. "Therefore, since we are surrounded by so great a cloud of witnesses, let us also lay aside every weight, and sin which clings so closely, and let us run with endurance the race that is set before us." Hebrew 12:1 I no longer had anything to hide. I felt cleansed, I felt so light. It taught me of His love and forgiveness that enabled me to show the same forgiveness and love to my earthly husband when he confessed to me his unfaithfulness and for my friend who became his OW for a time.

It was not just my marriage situation that He changed. He dealt with me about my selfishness, greed, childishness and contentiousness so I can be the godly wife He created me to be. He has been and still is changing and molding me into the Bride He wants me to be for Him. He replaced my fears with His blessed assurance that everything will be okay because He is with me always. From the broken and desperate woman I used to be, He healed me and made me whole again. I was no longer desperate to beg my earthly husband over and over or run after him. He gave me the faith to believe that in His perfect time, He would restore. I knew I just had to walk this journey with Him and watch as He brings to all His promises to pass His and find His will for my life.

I learned that I do not have to be afraid. He freed me my fears that held me back from living the life He wanted for me. Where I used to worry so much, He changed the way I used to think that now, I am able to have His peace in situations that would have made me anxious with worry, able to trust that He is in control. He has done a miracle in my life I never thought would happen in my lifetime—my Beloved restored my hearing!! Glory to God!!

Everyday is a reminder for me of His amazing grace as I hear every new sound and learn to appreciate this incredible blessing from Him. He is restoring other areas in my life as I learn to apply His truths. And I know He has only just begun!! I can't even begin to describe everything our precious Lord has done for me since my RJ started. I am in awe as I look back to the year and a half that together we walked this narrow path. He deserves all the glory, honor and praise due His mighty name!! It has truly been a life-changing journey and it doesn't end here!!

As I sought Him, He softened the heart of my earthly husband to continue to provide for me. Through my earthly husband and family, I never lacked for anything. He supplied ALL my needs once I learned to tithe to my storehouse, here at RMI.

By looking to the Lord instead of standing in my earthly husband's way, we continued to get along and to care for each other. My relationship with my earthly husband is such that we were able to talk about us, our situation, openly and still maintain our friendship even if things that hurt were said, things that made it clear our marriage was hopeless. I confess that often, this situation caused me to take my eyes off my Lord and brought me heartache. But in His mercy, He is always using this for good. I remember the times I really cried out to Him for deliverance and help in letting go.

Seeking Him with all my heart and mind, with all that I am and He changed things in an instant! Just as how He restored my marriage.

During my Restoration Journey, I learned about His everlasting love. One of the many life-changing truths I learned is His love for all of us. No one, NO ONE could ever love us as much as He does. And nothing can ever separate me from His love. No matter how many times I messed up, or how badly I did or will in the future, His love never changes. He will always be there to love me, accept me and hold my hand. Knowing the truth of how high and wide and deep and long is His love for us really helped me to open up my heart and let Him in. That He longs to know me too... it drew me to Him. It gave me that courage to not be afraid. He knows all my weakness, my sins, everything about me and He loves me just as I am.

Putting the Lord FIRST in my life and heart, for so long, was something I didn't know just how to do it. My flesh was weak and even then, my heart was not willing. I learned to keep asking and praying to Him to help me let go of my earthly husband and restoration. The process of letting go was one I continually have to learn throughout my RJ and especially now that I am restored. Because it was in letting go that allowed me to get to know who the Lord really is and how I will make it through the toughest times, being restored. By letting go of everything to run after the Lord, it blessed me with this amazing opportunity to know Him as my Beloved and have the intimate relationship I am now blessed to have with Him, which can never change or I will go backwards. It is worth every tear, every pain because knowing Him in this way gave me this anchor... this stronghold in my life, this knowledge that whatever happens, I will be okay because He loves me and I am His.

He is with me ALWAYS. He was the One holding my hand, giving me my strength, has been my stronghold in everything I faced. I didn't have to carry my burdens because I could cast my cares on Him because He cares for me. I honestly don't know how I would have gotten where I am now without Him. Knowing in my heart that He is always with me is so incredible. I am so blessed to experience His peace that surpasses all understanding that carried me through every refining fire. It is so humbling to look back now and see how far He taken me in our journey. It is all Him. Not anything I ever did. He carried me. He held my hand. Wow... I love You my Lord. Thank You. Thank You so much. I thank and praise you with all that I am.

Another thing I learned was about keeping quiet, having a gentle and quiet spirit and agreeing with my adversary quickly. This was a hard lesson for me to learn. I was so used to explaining and defending my side but by His grace and strength I am learning to die to myself. I learned that in the end, it doesn't really matter if I was able to say what I want because the Lord looks inside our hearts. Knowing that He knows the truth and that in His perfect time, His glory will be revealed made it easier for me to agree and let things go.

And who better to defend me than Him? He has shown me time and again that He is in control. No matter how hopeless a situation seems. No matter what is going on around me. And when our hearts condemns us, God is greater than our hearts and He knows everything. He has a purpose for everything that happens in our lives. That no matter what plans we make, it is the Lord's purpose that prevails. I really had to learn this truth in my heart and not lean on my own understanding. To be still and know that He is God and He will fight all my battles for me.

I used to be so materialistic, selfish and greedy. I treasured what was worthless and took for granted so many things. This journey opened my eyes to what is really important in life and showed me that everything I have is from Him. It is teaching me contentment. Learning to be content with what I have, where I am and in my situation, to give thanks always in everything. For every good and perfect gift is from above. And how amazing it is that He wants us, His brides, to have the best!! I am blessed to witness so many times how He gave me so much more that I could ever have imagined and requested in my wildest dreams!!

Along with my restoration, I am moving to the new house the Lord has blessed us with. When my earthly husband bought the house, I agreed to sign the papers my earthly husband asked me to, which stated I had no ownership of the house. Nevertheless, He covered me with His grace to accept it graciously, trusting that if this is the house He wants for our family, nothing could stop His plans. Never in all my life did I dare hope to live in such a house as we have. Only the Lord!! I am so grateful I know now that it's from Him and I pray to be able to rebuild our life and marriage on His rock, in His house. *Thank You for getting me ready for this test that you helped me pass.*

I also learned principle of tithing!! As I said before I can't stress enough that tithing to your storehouse FIRST is so important. I never had to worry about the enemy stealing from me because not only does

He promises to rebuke the devourer, but His blessings will overflow in your life!! And wow it did and continues to be in my life!! HE is faithful!! Test Him in this because you won't know what the enemy has stolen from you: your restoration, a new house?

One principle that was also important for me was confessing my sins especially my adultery to my earthly husband. I don't think I would be where I am if I never confessed or trusted in the Lord enough to believe in His promises. The enemy used my unconfessed sin to constantly bring me down and rob me of His peace. I am so thankful for my RJ who helped me to know the Lord to the point of being able to trust Him to this extent. He gave me the courage to confess. It was all the Lord. Without Him, I could never have done it.

It's true, we reap what we sow. Early on in my RJ, I had no intention of becoming a minister. All I wanted was for my marriage to be restored. But the Lord in His goodness had other plans, knowing what was best for me. He changed my heart to a heart that wants to help other women. He opened doors for me to volunteer in this ministry. I will always be grateful to the Lord for leading me to RMI. It changed my life in ways I never could have imagined. Being here was one of the things I loved most about my RJ. Thank You my Beloved!!

Late in my RJ, one of the most difficult times was when I had to really keep my mouth closed and agree with the hurtful things that were said when mocked for the choices I made to walk this narrow path. It intensified to the point I could only beg the Lord to release me, to flee to another place or if not, to give me the grace and strength to endure. As a result of this persecution, I found myself learning what it's like to really be content and accept His will to be done in my life. I remember clearly that day He changed things in an instant, when I laid down my will and was ready to accept and endure what is to come. That same day He heard my prayers and made plans for me to move to a different place to live, without me telling anyone anything!! He orchestrated it all. He is faithful!! My moving allowed me more time to commit to my ministry work and keep my eyes on the Lord. And I loved it!! My life revolved around Him and my work, that often I would get surprised when I hear from my earthly husband because he would be the last thing on my mind!! It's been one of the most rewarding experiences I have had and I'm so grateful for it.

Two months after I moved out of a bad living situation, my earthly husband has asked me to let go of my ministry work. I physically felt my heart ache. I love RMI so much, the Encouraging Women I was blessed to work with and who have become a part of my life, all that RMI does through and for the Lord. I don't know where I would be if it we're not for the Lord leading me to this ministry that changed my life. I honestly believed that I went through the worst already, but no. Letting go of RMI was the hardest yet the hardest I ever had to do in my RJ. It tested everything in me to submit and obey to my earthly husband. Even though it broke my heart, my Beloved was ever with me, giving me His strength and peace as I trust in what He has planned for me. My last day with RMI was the end of June. And of course RMI encouraged me to submit, to trust His plan, even though my leaving would cause additional work for everyone.

And I truly believe that the turning point was after I submitted to my earthly husband as unto the Lord in letting go of my ministry work, even though I didn't understand it then.

I shared above that my earthly husband and I would openly talk about our situation. It would start with light friendly conversation before we move on to serious things. It happened a few times in the 1 ½ year we have been separated and I never instigated it. I didn't push or begged him. I know from our conversations in the past that NOTHING I say will change his mind and that for me to push or beg would make it worse. Understanding it was NOT yet His appointed time. This was an area of weakness the Lord continued to deal with in me. Even though I knew the outcome, I would go there. Even if I already knew his answers, the stubbornness in me would still ask. But ONLY the Lord was able to turn his heart, in His perfect time. ONLY the Lord. Not me. Not anyone. So I know I should not have been asking my earthly husband. Please forgive me Lord. I thank You Lord so much even in my weakness, my foolishness, He always turned it for good because these situations that left me hurting (because I foolishly asked questions) caused me to always make me run to Him and seek His heart even more.

At this point in my RJ, I was content to wait on the Lord. I'd let to of RMI and my ministry work, allowing me to fully run after Him, wanting Him to be first in my life and heart. A week before my last day with RMI, my earthly husband and I talked about us again, with the same result as before. Afterwards, I cried to the Lord. I begged Him to help me let go completely. I begged Him to help me forget my earthly husband, something I never even prayed before. I wanted nothing more to do with my restoration. I wanted to be done and I just wanted move on. At that moment I felt every part of me ready and wanting to forget my earthly husband and move on.

Just as RMI says, once you really don't want restoration, when you beg Him to help you let go of everything and move on to be with Him, that's when it happens.

It happened the very next day, my earthly husband asked me what I never imagined he would, not after our conversation the night before, before I finally let go. My earthly husband was asking me to go with him to his family reunion!! Only the Lord!! He changed things in an instant!! The instant I was willing and able to finally let go of everything!!

My earthly husband flew me on the last day of June, right when my last day with RMI was supposed to be!! I am in awe of the timing of it all!! I hadn't seen my earthly husband for a year and this trip truly was a test for me in many ways. Applying everything I learned in my RJ and if I hadn't learned it the results would never have turned out as it did. The Lord helped me to see the areas He still needed to work in me and what I focused on when it was over. The Lord is so good!! He covered my nakedness when I was worried about how his family would accept me. But because of His great love for us, wow, I had the best time with his family, filled with acceptance and love they showered on both of us. It brings me to tears as I remember His goodness and amazing grace... Only my Beloved!! I had the most amazing time!! I only have praises for my Beloved as this trip also answered so many of my prayers I have prayed throughout my RJ. It didn't matter if we were not restored then, I had the best time on this trip and I was simply thankful and just as excited for what He had in store moving forward!

How my restoration finally happened was by me going on a family reunion trip with my earthly husband, I didn't know what to expect. I felt it was a chance for my earthly husband to see the changes the Lord has been doing in me. Being together again gave us a glimpse on how it would be like being with each other again. We both had a great time while staying in the house my earthly husband bought, we were able to joke and laugh about moving in together. But the question was left hanging if I should find a job there and move in with him. So when I asked my earthly husband about it, he asked for a few days to process it all, which was a surprise for me to say the least.

Sadly I confess that after the trip it was even harder for me to let go and be still. My earthly husband went from saying we are done, to rethinking about us again... even if he could not see the point of it all. My earthly husband's answers were different now; he no longer said we're "done" anymore. But he needed something more, something to make him want to try again and I knew it wasn't anything I could ever do or explain—Only the Lord could change his heart when it was time.

But even with this knowledge, I foolishly "helped" the Lord. A week after the trip, I asked my earthly husband again about the job situation, should I find a job where he lived. I let my flesh take over and pushed, asking my earthly husband if he would be willing for us to move in together. He emphatically said, "No. If I was I would have suggested it." Once again, that pain of rejection was a reminder for me to let go. But it was different this time, I hurt more from the fact that I proved I couldn't let go. After that, I expected not to hear from my earthly husband for a while.

I want so much to get to that place where the Lord is who I wanted more that anything. I wanted to be able to run after the Lord and for Him to become my everything. For the first time, I cried to the Lord for mercy. On my knees, I cried for Him to have mercy on me and help me forget my earthly husband, forget the trip we went on, forget the house I saw, forget any thoughts of what could be. **I just wanted Him to be my all in all.** I begged Him to help me forget about restoration entirely for the first time, and just to help me move on to what He had in store for the two of us, with just the Lord and me, alone.

That day I prayed for His grace and strength to help me do this. I know I could never do it on my own. And I determined not to contact earthly husband or answer his texts anymore, so I deleted his contact information from my phone. I kept going, I applied for jobs where I lived, determined to make a life for myself and move on with Him alone. I spent all morning the next day crying to Him, asking for forgiveness and mercy for never having let go fully. Writing to Him everything I felt and pouring out what was in my heart. That morning was the most difficult time in my RJ. Since my restoration's begun, I've had lots of bad news. I've gone through some horrible rejection and even learning about an OW being a close friend. But I had never felt hopeless. But I did this time. I felt the hopelessness, not by my situation but because of myself. I was tired of my weaknesses in holding on and I didn't know how I could ever let go enough not to stand in His way so He could fulfill His plans for my life. I didn't know how to let go so I could then pursue Him and only Him. So I kept begging Him to take everything away from me so He could have all of me, laying down my will, begging Him to show me how to love Him with all my heart, all my mind, all my soul and will with all my strength... I have never struggled so much as I did that morning.

And then it happened.

As I was talking to a dear sister, who has been holding up my hand like Aaron did for Moses, I was confessing to her of my hopelessness and feelings of wanting to give up on ever being able to move forward with the Lord as I wanted to do, when, I received a text from my earthly husband—a text I never thought I would get, especially not that day, not after what was said the night before. But there it was, he asked me when I was thinking of moving in. He was asking me when I want to move in!!!!

My Lord once again changed things in an instant!! Only the Lord knows what He saw in my heart. Truly, it was the last thing I expected that day. But oh, only Him!!!

My earthly husband left it up to me to pick the day I want to move in and he would buy my plane ticket. So I will finish out this month here and move in on the last day of the month there, with him. After a year and a half of separation, my Beloved is restoring my marriage. What I once thought was impossible proves... Nothing is truly impossible with the Lord. I love You my Lord!! I will sing praise to your name forever!!

There was a part of me that suspected I was close and His answers to my questions also made me sense it may be. Because the trials were getting harder and the events and timing of circumstances that happened made me think about I could be close. But my ways are not His ways, my thoughts not His thoughts, so I assumed I was wrong.

When we would talk about us, we were honest about how we felt, what was really in our hearts and it's then I could sense my earthly husband was torn. And from what he has opened up to me, he has said that he'd wanted so much to say 'yes' to us, but he didn't see the point. His responses have changed from we are "done" to leaving it up to what the future holds. That's when I knew then it was in the Lord's hands, not from what I say or did any more. It was not us, but the Lord who would restore our marriage. I just had to wait for His perfect timing and still as He continues to work and perfect His will and plan in our lives.

For anyone who is interested in changing their lives, which will lead to restoration, I would highly recommend the courses and pouring out your heart in your lesson forms. My courses helped me to open up my heart to Him and taught me His truths in a way that helped me to understand the truths so I could rebuild my life on His rock. The *How God can and will Restore your Marriage* book, *By the Word of Their Testimony* , Daily Devotionals—all their books and videos, I recommend!! I also recommend the Daily Encourager. Reading how the Lord is moving in each of our lives always encouraged me in my own journey.

When you have SG and are at the place in your RJ to let go of your need for church, and become His bride, I hope you will join Restoration Fellowship that will fill you with more of the Lord's amazing grace and love as you learn more about Him.

Would I be interested in helping encourage other women? Absolutely!!! *Yes my Lord!!* I'm hoping to return to ministering with RMI again, someday.

Dear Brides,

When my marriage fell apart, I never imagined it was the Lord trying to get my attention. I must admit this was the hardest thing I ever had to go through. The trials were heartbreaking and difficult. But these trials and the trials that will come in your life are being used to refine us, to mold and shape us to be the godly wife He created us to be, so when He restores our marriage, we are ready for it, ready to rebuild our marriage to one that will last, because it is founded on His Rock and He will be eternally glorified. Learn it now, because the tests get harder, if not, you won't make it.

I can honestly say now that I would not change a thing. I am so blessed to have come out so much better after all this. And YOU WILL too. I found answers I have been looking for, answers I didn't even know I needed. This season led me to finding the Lover of my Soul that filled every void in my life, filling me with His joy, His peace, His amazing grace and a Love like no other. It is truly amazing and I cannot wait for you to experience this life-changing journey with the Lord. I am blessed to learn that this is not just a journey to find marriage restoration, but more importantly, a journey of restoration us to our First Love, the best Husband there is! Your life will no longer be that empty void, simply existing but one full of meaning, complete and wanting nothing. All because of Him.

Spend this season in your life getting to know the Lord intimately, looking to Him for everything, making Him FIRST in your life and heart. Let go and run after the Lord. Throughout my RJ, I found time and again that when I truly let go in my heart is when He moved each time on my behalf and changed things in an instant.

Our Beloved looks inside our hearts. Nothing we *say* will ever change anyone's mind. Only the Lord can turn the situation around and turn our earthly husband's heart back to us. He is the One who will restore our marriage. Not us. So if you are like me, who struggles with letting go, ask Him to help you, beg for Him to do it in you. Ask Him to show you how because He is faithful!!

Nothing is impossible with the Lord. No heart is too hard for Him. No situation is too difficult. He can and will restore your marriage in His perfect time. What He did for me, He will do for you too. So enjoy this time of waiting as you seek Him with all your heart. He will become so real to you that your life will never be the same! He loves you, dear Brides. He longs to give you the desires of your hearts. And He will. As you take His hand and walk with Him in this journey, He will show you how wide and long and high and deep His love is for you!! He will do immeasurably more than you can ever imagine!! So trust, believe and wait in hope for the Lord.

~ *Joy in Nevada* was our very beautiful Tagalog translator, who has experienced freedom after embracing His truths. Even though Joy was deaf when she first arrived, while with us the Lord used her in amazing ways until her husband contacted her to meet him. After letting go of her Marriage Restoration and her church Joy now says "I live a fear-free, worry-free life!" even though she has no idea what her future holds. Then the impossible happened, after 25 Years, she could hear!

Chapter 3

I thought I Should be Respected

"And let the wife see to it that
she respect her husband."
—Ephesians 5:33

I discovered RMI almost 2 years ago. At that time I'd been with my husband for 8 1/2 years. I accepted Jesus as my Lord and Savior at a young age; therefore, I knew for God to bless our union we needed to be married. We already had 2 children together prior to our marriage so we were married first by a civil ceremony, then later we were married by a Christian pastor.

Looking back were always problems, but I never truly surrendered them to God. I noticed a distancing from both me and my husband soon after we were married, prior to that I felt nothing could ever separate us because we were best friends. But I also remember my mother telling me that once I was married, the devil would attack our marriage.

So, it began with us distancing, then fighting and then dis-respectfulness. That's when my husband asked me to leave "his" house back to the U.S. I would tell him the problem was that **he** didn't love me anymore. I would back down, I was proud and would tell him I was not going to let him treat me badly. He'd then apologize for asking me to leave.

Then the fatal blow was when we went to a marriage counselor. Because my husband wouldn't fully open up and. e stopped going, my counselor told me I knew I needed to leave for the sake of my kids and that I also knew deep inside he was cheating on me.

I'd told her my husband had begun to lie all the time and told me I was controlling; therefore, he would no longer tell me where he was going and asked I didn't call when he was gone. Though he would always come home at night and he was always kind to the children but unfortunately one day while I was sobbing I called a Christian older lady I knew, and she told me God told her for me to leave and never come back to his country.

So since my marriage counselor told me to leave as well and because my husband was one of the most difficult cases she said she ever dealt with (she said he had no morals, that he was arrogant and liked being like that and that he was incapable of loving, and that he was also *capable* of physically abusing me). So, I foolishly took that as a sign. I told my husband my 2 kids and I would be traveling to the U.S. on vacation for a month or so.

When he would call me, he was very rude and cruel on the phone, he would ask when I was bringing his kids back home. I would tell him soon, maybe in a few weeks. The truth I was scared to go back home, I felt hatred from my husband and I was very depressed. Because I never sought the Lord but sought help from others. I knew nothing of what the Bible said and felt I was who should be respected.

Even before I left his country, I thought of suicide, so I was scared to go back to that.

Then, one day he said he had heart problems, but didn't want me coming unless I was bringing the kids, but because I didn't know how to trust the Lord, I was still too afraid. I thought that if I went back, he could divorce me and keep the kids in his country.

The final tearing down of my house was when I asked if he was cheating and he said no. But because I wasn't trusting the Lord and didn't trust him, I looked through his phone for the first time and found a girl on his call log every night, and found their text messages. When I heard him on the phone after we had a random fight, he screamed at me in public (he had never done that before) and after much probing and crying he admitted he was cheating on me, first he told me he felt bad for her and wanted us to try working on our marriage—but the tables turned just like Erin says in her book. Soon I was crying and begging him not to leave me and the kids! I went so far as to tell him to kill me!!

Once I calmed down, he told me he it was my fault for leaving him for 8 months, and that's when his feelings had died. He said he had become bitter but was now happy with her. He said he loved his kids and me, just not in a way a man should love a wife. He said it was over. Even though I begged and begged, he said it was over.

That's when he proposed we stay living in the same house and that he wouldn't divorce me, which meant that I could keep his last name, but that he would never leave the other woman. The final push was when I let my flesh take over and I called the OW and even lied to my husband about how I got her phone number.

That's when I broke down and prayed to God that He would forgive my sinning ways and for meddling in His plans. I left to a hotel for one night so my kids wouldn't see the mess I was in but mostly so I could dedicate time to seeking God and His perfect will. I returned back home, but things are awkward between my husband (we are being cordial with each other) and as soon as I surrendered my situation and life and family and husband to God He led me to you.

Two years later I emailed Restoration Fellowship, my church without walls, with this email:

I just wanted to update you on my marriage situation. As you know shortly after joining the RMI Translation Team, I took a leave of absence because I felt the Lord told me He was preparing me for the restoration of my marriage after about 2 years of struggles.

Honestly, It's been a "harder than I thought" final battle especially because I had already felt so much peace in my life since the LORD had become my center. The hardest test was last five months ago where I nearly gave it all up because I thought why keep on if my life is great with the LORD. I just don't need this restoration to be happy. However, I believed in the promises of my Lord and Savior and Heavenly Husband and the blessings I believed He had in store for my family.

A month into my last battle, and after I told the Lord I didn't need restoration to be happy, my earthly husband started being nicer and nicer and taking me out more. We always stayed living in the same home as he'd said we would, but this is when I noticed he no longer went out or stayed out late. Also, instead of him being upset or annoyed with me, he started being more playful and communicating with me.

Yet, the battle was far from over, near the end of the restoration month things began to get crazy. I started seeing text messages and phone calls from the OW again, so I decided (while not being emotional at all but keeping completely calm and peaceful), that I didn't want to continue in my marriage restoration journey. Of course, I went to Him many times about this and felt at total peace with my decision to only be His bride. Nevertheless, I did pray that if was His will for me to continue to stay in my marriage, to please help me see that because I didn't want it anymore.

That's when I felt led to share this with my husband. So I approached my earthly husband in a caring, loving and peaceful way I told him that I liked how great our relationship was but that I would like to continue my life without him as my husband. But, this letting go changed everything, the Lord is so faithful and amazing. In a very calm way, my earthly husband told me that he was no longer with the OW and he asked what *he* could do. I replied, "I'm not asking you to do anything; I just like our relationship as parents just the way it is." That's when my earthly husband explained that he was speaking with the OW, so that she would not call him again because he didn't care about ever having any communication with her and that he would delete her number from his phone. He told me he wanted us to be at peace, and I told him we are at peace though. So he reiterated that he wanted us to be in peace but as a family together!

I now realize, that I had been praying for several months for God to let me know the relationship with the OW was over, and He was answering my prayer. I do believed He allowed this for good so I could have my confirmation and since I never dared mentioned her before because I wasn't sure if my earthly husband still had something going on with the her. Yes, God works in mysterious ways.

Let me close by saying it's definitely true what Pastor Erin says, once we truly let go and let God have His way and complete His plan...when we are truly in the most intimate and loving relationship with the LORD and prove that He's first. When we realize we don't have to *try* loving and knowing Lord...it just happens...without us try, we can fall so in love with Him that nothing else matters. It's only when we can really walk away from even praying for a restoration in our marriage...THAT'S when it just happens.

Let me say like so many others, God is good all the time and all the time God is good.

Thanks to You to God and to my Lord and to everyone at RMI for sticking by me and helping me through this process. I pray that all who approach RMI will truly find a relationship with our Heavenly Husband who longs for us and will never leave us. God bless you all!

────────────Chapter 4────────────

RESTORED Marriage & Baby

"With the imperishable quality of a
gentle and quiet spirit,
which is precious in the sight of God."
—1 Peter 3:4

Shasha, tell us how did your restoration actually begin?

After two years of separation from my earthly husband, my marriage
was restored that included a restoration baby!

**How did God change your situation as you sought Him
wholeheartedly?**

My restoration journey lasted one year and ten months to be exact.
Although for the first year my relationship with my heavenly
Husband grew to higher heights of intimacy, it was only two months
before my marriage was restored which is when I had finally and
completely let go of my earthly husband. I had the reach the point
where I would I tell my sweet Lord that if he restored my marriage I
would be happy, but if he decided not to, I would be just as happy and
continue to serve him all the days of my life.

**What principles, from God's Word (or through our resources),
did the Lord teach you during this trial?**

My sweet heavenly Husband taught me that His love for me is greater
than the love of any other human being. I learnt that if I had to to be a
true bride that I had to deny myself of every fleshly desire and follow
Him and His lead. That my love for Him must be so great that when
compared to the love that I have for my earthly husband, mother
father, siblings, and other loved ones, it would seem like hate.

From this ministry, I learnt so many amazing and mind-blowing principles. I learnt what it meant to be a virtuous woman with a gentle and quiet spirit. I also learnt what it meant to truly let go of my situation and my marriage and allow the Lord to become my everything. My heavenly Husband filled me with so much joy, happiness, and peace that many people were not even aware of my situation. My face was radiant as I continued to seek my Love.

What were the most difficult times that God helped you through?

The most difficult time that my sweet heavenly Husband helped me through was the embarrassment that I faced in work seeing that my earthly husband daily since we worked in the same place. Also, my heavenly Husband filled the loneliness in my life and He replaced my fear with a spirit of trust and peace.

What was the "turning point" of your restoration?

Even though my earthly husband and I were always in contact and would go out on dates during my restoration journey, the actual turning point of my restoration was just two months before my restoration when I truly let go of my earthly husband and my marriage. At that exact moment my heavenly Husband turned everything around and then we were even blessed with a restoration baby. As I write this I am now three and half months pregnant!!! All glory to my Lord!

Tell us HOW it happened? Did your husband just walk in the front door?

My earthly husband started to seek me out more and more as the days passed as soon as I completely let go. He began texting and calling often, inviting me out frequently on dates, and complimenting me on many occasions. He also expressed his confusion about his pursuing the divorce. Then we found out that we were pregnant but he still said that married or divorce, that we would be the best parents possible to this baby. At that time I had not moved back in permanently to live with him. I was still going back and forth at his request. Two weeks after being back and forth, my earthly husband declared that he loved me and wanted to spend the rest of his life with me and no longer wanted the divorce. Soon after, he asked me to move back home. Thank you my sweet sweet Lord!

Did you suspect or could you tell you were close to being restored?

Yes I suspected but only as I drew closer to my heavenly Husband, and that's when my earthly husband drew closer to me and started to pursue me more. Again, this is not something that can be faked. It must be genuine.

Would you recommend any of our resource in particular that helped you?

The resources that helped me the most were: How God can and will Restore your Marriage and definitely the A Wise Woman book. Also all the RRR online courses, The Praise Reports, and the daily Encouragers. Thank you so much to Erin and the other members of this ministry for making these resources available to me!

Would you be interested in helping encourage other women?
Yes! I came here after being involved in part of Rejoice Ministries and it was here I learned to take my eyes off of everything and put it on Him so I could experience His love.

Either way, what kind of encouragement would you like to leave women with in conclusion?

Seek the Lord first. You cannot fake or pretend. The Lord looks at our hearts, our souls, and other thoughts. Do not focus on the faults of anyone else, but examine yourselves and ask your heavenly Husband to change you into that virtuous woman.

Additionally, you must come to the point that your are contented being with your heavenly Husband and no one else. Come to the place where anything but Him no longer is your focus, no longer on earthly matters, but rather on what your heavenly Husband desires of and for you.

Also, give of yourself, your prayers, and your time to others, not focusing on yourself, giving them the same comfort you receive from your heavenly Husband, be sure share it with others who are hurting. Most importantly, the LORD must always be first place in your life.

~ Shasha in Tobago

---------------Chapter 5---------------

ANY Marriage can be Saved!!

"But God chose the foolish things
to shame the wise;
God chose the weak things
to shame the strong."
—1 Corinthians 1:27

Kopano please tell us, how did your restoration actually begin?

Before I actually begin I want to tell you that I was the foolish of the foolish, and many people often feel pity for me because I am so tiny in frame (often mistaken for a teenager) that when I was faced with marital problems and divorce, people felt such pity because as small as I am, and what I was going through, to others, looked like too much trouble for such a tiny person!

1 Corinthians 1:27 NIV "But God chose the foolish things of the world to shame the wise; God chose the weak things of the world to shame the strong."

My husband and I first met by chance over the lunch hour in the area where we both worked (different organizations but same area). It would be about 2 months after that that we began dating. Upon return from our first dinner date, I texted my best friend at that time, "I think I've met my husband" and shortly after, my husband (then boyfriend) texted me, "My life has just become beautiful."

3 months later I was pregnant with our first daughter,he proposed and I accepted. We were married 5 months later.

Now, I had given my life to the Lord 6 years earlier while at university in South Africa and had had such a wonderful relationship with Him while at university often telling my friends that I couldn't even imagine having a boyfriend because my Lord occupied every area of my life that there was no room for a boyfriend.

I had asked the Lord not to send me back to my country when I completed my degree, but He did and that had made me so angry that I told Him outright that I was angry and I began to backslide. So my being pregnant here was as a result of my having backslidden and began living in immorality.

I knew however that this was wrong, and this was the first point of difficulty with the relationship and what would become one of the main issues throughout the relationship thereafter. Although I was engaging in sexual relations with my husband (boyfriend at the time), I battled with knowing I was living in sin and was never at peace with this. My husband, though he believed in God, did not have a personal relationship with the Lord and could not understand why I would always be talking about how bad it was that I was doing this and it just made the whole thing unpleasurable for him. I confused him because I'd say I shouldn't do what we were doing, and the next thing, I'd be the one leading him to it.

Even after we got married, where now I should have been freer to do that, we both were never free about it because of all the history and so this contributed to the suffering of our marriage.

Why did I begin by saying I was the foolish of the foolish? Because my husband never cheated on me; he was devoted to our family, he always made sure I knew where he was without me asking. He was loyal to me first before his family (he had really left and cleaved to me), he spent his earnings for our home and not for anything else. In short, my husband never really did anything that should have led to where we would later find ourselves.

I on the other hand LOVED to analyze every little situation and was so controlling and critical; e.g. if my husband was not reading the Bible with me, it was bad for the marriage. If he was not praying with me, it was bad for the marriage; if he was not calling my mother as often as I thought he should, I'd give him grief about it, and on and on. I carried on with criticizing him at every turn. I again had absolutely no respect for any authority, not my husband, not my superiors at work, not anyone. I was the MOST CONTENTIOUS WOMAN EVER, all my life growing up, I was known for being argumentative and contentious, and I knew it. Everyone knew it and spoke about it, but we all thought it meant I was assertive. I thought I

was the most intelligent woman ever and thought my husband should
actually be happy about my intellect etc. And to top it all, I was a
judgmental, hypocritical pharisee who spent much time studying the
beliefs of all various denominations and religions and then spent more
time criticizing them saying how they either were cults or didn't know
how to interpret the Bible. Can you believe that all that I'm saying I
was, my husband had time and time again pointed out to me and I said
to him that I didn't see anything wrong with it!

My husband warned me of the following throughout my marriage:

1. I need to be careful with my words, he said this exact sentence,
"words are very powerful. Choose your words carefully".

2. He warned me that I was not submissive and that I needed to allow
him as my husband to lead me. I told him plainly that no, I would
never do it.

3. He warned me that I was contentious and argumentative and that it
made him withdraw from me. I said to him I cannot just agree with
everything he says if I didn't believe the same things.

4. My husband even went as far as lovingly telling me to find an older
woman to teach me about being a wife, but I flat out said no and said
he should find an older man to teach him how to be a husband!

So, I'm pointing this out to show you that I was the foolish of the
foolish because unlike many women who say that their husbands just
upped and left them without warning that it was actually THEY that
were the problem, I was plainly warned and if I had been wise, I
would have cried out to God to help me, but no, I was very prideful.
My husband didn't jump into adultery, instead he tried to teach me
these same principles that I have now been learning through RMI but
I was a fool and never listened!

Because I couldn't see my own sin, but ALWAYS was criticizing my
husband, childish in every way, always demanding that he do things
just how I wanted him to, never allowing him to lead but wanting to
lead him, he withdrew and became very distant and I became so
unhappy, believing that he didn't love me anymore and often accusing
him of this. He didn't bother to try to convince me otherwise but
withdrew   more   and   eventually   stopped   talking   to   me

ALTOGETHER! I discovered just after the beginning of his total shut down that I was pregnant with our second child and thought surely my husband would now talk to me since I was pregnant - wrong. My husband stared at me blankly with absolutely no response when I told him the news.

About 3 weeks into this silence, I dragged my husband to counselling which he attended only because it was with a pastor he respected, so he didn't want to disrespect him by not pitching up. If it were not for that, he would never have come because at this stage, he had completely checked out of the marriage.

Counselling made things a lot worse as I heard my husband declare that he had clearly married the wrong woman! I was crushed. When my husband had first met me, he had gone around telling everyone that I was THE ONE and had even bought me a perfume called THE ONE! Now he was saying the opposite!

We stopped counselling immediately after that session and I went online and enrolled into a secular marriage help programme that borders on new age teachings for about $1000. It promised to be the ultimate solution and I believed it. When nothing changed, I knew my marriage was over. My husband would still not even say hi to me, though we still lived in the same house and slept on the same bed.

Again, I was the foolish of the foolish, so I decided to move out of our home! I could no longer bear the silence, and I contacted a divorce lawyer to find out if I could legally move out of the house with our daughter. She said yes, so I packed up and moved out to a rented house determined to get a divorce.

About 2 weeks after this, I woke up from my sleep hearing this question right at the core of me, "If you don't pray for your husband, who will?" Again the following night, and what I believe must have been the Holy Spirit filling me with such power and fervency to pray, day and night, even whilst driving.

I didn't know at the time that it would be 10 whole months before God would answer my prayers because it was He who had "removed friend, lover and acquaintances far from me" because I had forsaken my first Love.

How did God change your situation as you sought Him wholeheartedly?

Over the 10 months of my husband wanting nothing to do with me at all, I sought and sought for help. Church couldn't help me; I went to a church where the pastor is also a prophet, but God gave no prophecies regarding my marriage!

I went online, found a popular "standers" ministry and received so much hope for my marriage, but unfortunately it didn't teach me Biblical principles on how to allow God to restore marriage, so my situation didn't improve.

One day, 8 months into the separation, I knelt down before the Lord and said, "Lord, there's no change in my situation at all. I'm tired of being in the same place in the desert, let's move to another phase, another level." 2 days later I stumbled upon RMI and when I read THIS IS YOUR DIVINE APPOINTMENT. GOD HAS HEARD YOUR CRY, I knew it was my answer!

I devoured what I read, non-stop for 2 weeks on my cellphone before I had a computer and before starting the courses. I immediately applied the principles, stopped ALL attempts to contact my husband and did nothing in the flesh any longer.

When RMI said it was the Lord who had removed my husband, I immediately remembered my university days when the Lord was all I wanted and needed and lived for, and how I had left Him and backslid and I knew it was true that He had removed my husband so that I'd go back to Him, my first Husband, as He once had been. And because I'd previously "tasted this and knew that the Lord was good", I desperately sought Him to revive the relationship we had together at university. I'd pray and say, "Lord, I know what Erin means, I experienced this before, please let's go back there, please." I'd say, and still say to Him, "give me the same type of relationship with You as You have with Erin."

Very soon I was falling so madly in love with Him that I no longer wanted restoration and actually stopped doing my daily lessons! I then felt the urge to fast and seek Him about this and He put me back on the road to restoration by reminding me why He had initially put in my heart to turn away from seeking divorce.

Instead of returning me to my lessons, He led me to purchase the *Facing Divorce* book, little did I realize that only a few days later I'd be receiving divorce papers!!! So when I received them, I knew just what to do—I fell flat on my face and praised Him. Literally, all that came out of my mouth was praise and this was the turning point in my restoration.

What principles, from God's Word (or through our resources), did the Lord teach you during this trial?

To be quiet. To speak only kindly. To submit to my husband and all authority. To let go of my church and become His church, His bride. To bring the whole tithe to my storehouse (that made such a huge difference in my moving forward) and so many more principles I can't name them all.

What were the most difficult times that God helped you through?

Going through all 9 months of pregnancy without my husband, with him not even talking to me. The me delivering the baby totally without him taking any interest was by far the most difficult. Yet, by God's grace, my husband is now very involved with our daughter and loves her to bits!

What was the "turning point" of your restoration?

My husband filing for divorce. Thankfully after reading the *Facing Divorce* book, I was ready and knew what to do and followed the principles. I knew that in these principles lay my miracle so I was very careful to read the *Facing Divorce* book again to make sure I didn't violate any principles.

So I agreed quickly, did not obtain a lawyer, met with my husband and his lawyer on my own, and although there were untrue things in the papers and I was basically going to be walking away with nothing, not even one car (though we had 3 cars). Instead of saying anything of what I wanted or needed, I exclaimed that the offer they had made me was very generous and I said I was thankful. I think this baffled them both! When asked to sign the papers I signed without hesitation. The lawyer asked how I felt and I said I was happy for my husband because he deserved to be happy.

Tell us HOW it happened? Did your husband just walk in the front door?

After this meeting with my husband and the lawyer, I continued to pray against the divorce, but not too fervently because I really knew that no matter what the outcome would be, I was going to be fine because I have a Husband anyway.

One day it was impressed on me to look up Philippians 4:5 which says, Let your gentleness be evident to all. The Lord is near. Then it was impressed on me to look up four verse in a specific order. I didn't know these verses at all:

Philippians 4:5 "Let your gentleness be evident to all. The Lord is near."

Galatians 4:5 "…to redeem those under the law, that we might receive adoption to sonship."

1 Corinthians 4:5 "Therefore judge nothing before the appointed time; wait until the Lord comes. He will bring to light what is hidden in darkness and will expose the motives of the heart. At that time each will receive their praise from God."

2 Corinthians 4:5 "For what we preach is not ourselves, but Jesus Christ as Lord, and ourselves as your servants for Jesus' sake."

1 Thessalonians 4:5 "not in the passion of lust like the Gentiles who do not know God."

So when I put them together it read:

"Let your gentleness be evident to all. The Lord is near. To redeem those under the law, that we might receive adoption to sonship. Therefore judge nothing before the appointed time; wait until the Lord comes. He will bring to light what is hidden in darkness and will expose the motives of the heart. At that time each will receive their praise from God. For what we preach is not ourselves, but Jesus

Christ as Lord, and ourselves as your servants for Jesus' sake. Not in the passion of lust like the Gentiles who do not know God. "

I pondered over this and asked the Lord what it meant, but got no answer.

2 DAYS LATER my husband, who loathed me and had not spoken to me for 10 months called and said he was at my gate. He proceeded to tell me to fight for the marriage, that he couldn't believe I agreed to the divorce without fighting, that I needed to consider our small children that they needed an unbroken family and their father. LOL! Unbelievable! I respectfully said, yes, ok.

A week later he came again (2 weeks before the court date) and asked me to move in with him. So, now I am slowly moving my things to his house and sleep there every night now. It's been just a few days but very wonderful days. I have matured and we are enjoying our relationship and family.

Did you suspect or could you tell you were close to being restored?

Absolutely not. The hate wall was incredibly strong all throughout up to the day my husband came to say he didn't want a divorce anymore. In fact, the night before he'd come to drop off our daughter he hardly said a sentence to me. Other people say they could be intimate with their spouses and I always wondered how because in my situation my husband loathed me so much that could never even have been a possibility of happening. For the entire 10 months!

Would you recommend any of our resource in particular that helped you?

Yes. EVERYTHING! *How God can and will Restore your Marriage* book. The RRR online courses. Be Encouraged videos. *A Wise Woman*, *Facing Divorce*. Then read *Facing Divorce* again. Though I didn't complete my online courses, I read all of the lessons over and over and the Lord is leading me to redo Course 1 "At Last There's Hope" and work through as recommended in the ministry.

In fact, what I recommend is to daily read at least one chapter of *A Wise Woman* or *How God can and will Restore your Marriage* book even after restoration. To continue reading them DAILY along with the daily Bible readings. I still read these EVERY DAY WITHOUT FAIL.

Would you be interested in helping encourage other women?

Absolutely.

What kind of encouragement would you like to leave women with in conclusion?

After my experience I know that ANY marriage can be saved. Just believe it and receive it. But above all, take the Lord as your Husband. He is charming!

There's lots more wonderful things He did for me during my RJ but they are too many to tell.

John 21:25 NIV "Jesus did many other things as well. If every one of them were written down, I suppose that even the whole world would not have room for the books that would be written."

~ *Kopano in Namibia*

Chapter 6

Restored after Daughter Shot

"I can do all this through Him
who gives me strength."
—Philippians 4:13

"In My Favor"

Though my circumstances are less than favorable, I just praise God that He's taking me through this journey because sooner or later, it'll turn in my favor!!

In the wee hours of the night, my car was repo'd due to nonpayment. I've been going through so many financial struggles but I never lost hope in God and His word, for He is my Provider!!! 2 Cor. 9:8 "And God is able to make all grace abound to you, so that in all things at all times, having all that you need, you will abound in every good work." Even though I had been praying for God to provide me with the finances to make a payment, I didn't receive all of it and my car was taken. But praise be to the Almighty God for this storm!!! I know that I am going through this because He loves me and I am His!!

James 1:3-4 "... because you know that the testing of your faith develops perseverance. Perseverance must finish it's work so that you may be mature and complete, not lacking in anything." Peter already warned us that we will go through trials (1 Peter 4:12-13). For that, I give God the glory for forming me into who He needs me to be through my trials and circumstances!! I will continue to build my foundation on His word and believe that He will not take me where His grace can't save me!! I am not letting my situation discourage me!

God is doing a mighty work in me because I'm not focused on my earthly husband, I'm focused on my relationship with my heavenly Husband and how I can be HIS bride!!! He is filling me with a kind and gentle spirit who smiles at the future :). In the natural realm, this may not seem like much to praise God for, but I'm offering all the praises to Him because even though I can't see the victory, I know that it is already won! I once believed that my situation was hopeless, but nothing is too hard for God!!!!! (Jer. 32:27)

"Praise Him in the Storm"

My desire has always been to write a PR that would uplift women and to encourage them as I've been encouraged. I always felt as though a PR should be written if you have a testimony or if God has provided a supernatural miracle. Well, my praise is caused by none of those. I lift up and exalt the Mighty Name of my Lord and Savior and give Him all the praise because He is worthy! I shout Hallelujah because He deserves the highest praise!! There is NONE like Him.

Through my struggles, I've heard the enemy whisper, "Where is your God now"? To the natural eyes, it may even seem as if God is nowhere to be found. I've taken a huge pay cut from my job, I can barely keep up with my bills, my car is going to be repossessed, things between my earthly husband and I have not gotten better, and I'm about to be evicted from my apartment. I write this PR with tears in my eyes because I don't know how God is going to turn this situation around in such a short time. I don't even know if He will change my circumstances. I praise Him because I am standing on His word and promise for me!!!

"I can do all this through Him who gives me strength." (Phi 4:13)

No matter what I go through, He is there!! He is an ever-present help in trouble, whose grace is sufficient for me in my time of weakness!!! He is my source, my strength, my life and without Him I am NOTHING!! I know whose I am and I can rest in the comfort of knowing I am a child of God regardless of the storm I'm in, "because the Lord disciplines those He loves, and He chastens everyone He accepts as His child!" (Heb 12:6). All things will work together and I just wanted to encourage everyone who's hurting right now to look to God!! Build your foundation on His word!! He will NEVER leave you nor forsake you and He will never take you where His grace can't save you! Tears are flowing down my face as I meditate on His goodness. I'm not out of it yet, but I thank Him for the peace He has rested in my heart. I'm not going to wait until I'm out of it. I'm going to praise Him in advance!!! "Rejoice in the Lord always. I will say it again: Rejoice!" (Phi 4:4)

"No Limits"

The enemy had me believe his lies that my God was nowhere near. I almost gave up on Him and this ministry. On this exact day, a day where I felt nothing but despair and discouragement, I decided to read the Encourager, "Praise Him in the Storm." I knew it was God leading me to read it because I don't normally read it this early in the morning. He used my very own PR to encourage me! He reminded me of the peace I once had and revealed that my peace and joy lies in Him! If I wanted to be delivered, I had to seek Him! If I wanted to be changed, I had to seek Him! If I needed encouragement, I had to seek Him!!

Ladies, HE IS THE KEY! HE IS THE ANSWER!! No matter what we're going through or where we might currently find ourselves, it's not over!! When God is in it, there is NO limits. Make Him your refuge. Make your worship to Him your dwelling place. Seek Him with all your heart and He WILL make Himself known to you. Praise the Most High God!! Lord You are Worthy!! Thank You for being a God who lacks in nothing.

"So remember this and keep it firmly in mind: The Lord is God both in heaven and on earth, and there is no other." Deuteronomy 4:39 NLT

"A Way out of No Way"

All things work together for the good of them that love the Lord!! I shout praises unto my heavenly Husband for no one can do what You do! I am overwhelmed with joy because I know that I am His!

I have been out of a job for a couple of months now and it has been a struggle to pay my bills, to eat and I cannot drive due to my tags being expired and having no funds to get insurance. But my Lord always makes a way out of no way! The enemy constantly uses my finances to bring me down. When this happens, I meditate on His word and listen to His still, small voice that says "Come to me and I will give you rest". I put all of my burdens at His throne and asked Him to take control and He did!

I recall days where I would lay on the floor with my face buried on the ground and I would just lay everything at His feet. Time and time again, He has shown me that His grace is sufficient enough for me and that His strength is made perfect in my weakness. PTL!

Three weeks ago, I enrolled in an online school and I was scheduled to receive a refund from financial aid. Praise be to the true and living God, my refund was over twice than my scheduled amount AND my refund came 10 days earlier than the scheduled date!

Who else but God!!! He is always on time and when He shows up, He always shows out!!

My Marriage is RESTORED!!!

So, Jazmin, how did your restoration actually begin?

My restoration has been long overdue, but I feel it is working exactly in my Heavenly Husband's timing :)

My husband and I have been together for almost 10 years and married for 2 years, although we have been separated longer than we have been able to enjoy our marriage. The trouble first started on the day of our marriage. We didn't have a traditional wedding, but instead opted to have a court wedding with just us and the officiate. We were to have dinner to celebrate later that evening when my husband accused me of scheming to plan the dinner when I knew he wanted to watch basketball.This took me by complete surprise because the entire dinner was his idea. Needless to say, we did not celebrate our marriage.

This was such a shock because before we got married, things were amazing between my husband and I. We were planning on buying a house and talked about having another child once we got married. Once we got married, however, everything began to spiral down from there, and from that moment on, I knew the enemy was going to do whatever it took to sabotage our union. We married two years after our daughter was shot. Though she recovered, I am sure it took its toll on both of us.

It was only a week after we got married when my husband told me he no longer wanted any kids and did not want to focus on buying a house. This caused us to argued constantly, mostly from me feeling neglected, his smoking and him coming home in the early hours of the morning.

Then in September, my husband left and said he no longer wanted to be with me. Thankfully, a week later he recanted and told me he wanted to do whatever it takes to make our marriage work so we decided to get some counseling from my pastor, which made things worse.

During our first session, my husband informed my pastor and I that he no longer wanted the marriage anymore and he didn't know why he decided to get counseling. A couple of days after, we got into a huge argument when my husband threw his wedding ring outside and said he was getting a divorce.

For days, I made the mistake of begging him to work things out but to no avail. Then one day in December, I had a dream that my husband was in adultery. I woke up in a cold sweat and was going through a panic attack. I called him and asked him if he had been unfaithful to which he denied. The next month I found emails in my account (his email was accidentally synced to my account) where he was propositioning women. I asked him again if he had been unfaithful and he admitted he was a couple of weeks before I had asked him the first time. I was devastated, but I knew that God did not want me to file for divorce. I tried to find every reason and excuse to justify me wanting a divorce and that's when God led me to RMI.

The day I found RMI I immediately began applying the principles and slowly started to see the changes in my husband. A year after our separation, our marriage was temporarily restored, for about four months, when my husband left again.

How did God change your situation as you sought Him wholhusbandeartedly?

When my husband left me the second time, I immediately knew that God was trying to get my attention. When my marriage was restored the first time, I realized I became a contentious woman yet again. I no longer applied the principles I learned from RMI and my relationship with my Heavenly Husband soon began to fade. That's when He lovingly removed lover and friend far from me again so that I can focus on returning to my first love, Him. The first time around, during my Restoration Journey, I focused on the restoration itself. But during my second RJ, I solely focused on reconnecting with my First Love. I was overcome with such peace that joy that surpassed all understanding. I no longer *longed* for my husband and I no longer prayed for our restoration. Instead, I prayed for his salvation and four months later my husband returned back home!

What principles, from God's Word (or through our resources), did the Lord teach you during this trial?

The Lord showed me that He is all I need. He revealed to me that I was still a contentious woman and that my focus needs to be on Him, not my husband. Through RMI's resources, I applied the very important principle of keeping my mouth shut! I agreed with my adversary and focused on having a gentle and quiet spirit. I believe the most important principle I have applied, though, is tithing. Through my first RJ, my husband did not help me out at all. The second time around, at the moment I began tithing, my heavenly Husband supplied all of my needs! Though I am not working, He has made sure that all of my bills are paid and that there is food on the table. He has led my husband and family members to help me out without me even asking them!!

What were the most difficult times that God helped you through?

The most difficult times were when my daughter would pray for her dad to come home and to change his ways and stop doing drugs. It was hard to see that my daughter was at the point that she understood what was going on and knew that her father's smoking was bad and knew that when he did; he was a different person. It was also difficult when I did not see the answer to my prayers when I asked God to change my husband. My heavenly Husband has helped me through this by reminding me that He is no respecter of persons and that "The king's heart is like a stream of water directed by the LORD; he guides it wherever he pleases". I know that if He has done it for me, then He can do it for anyone.

What was the "turning point" of your restoration?

I believe the turning point was after I had been restored. The RF Office sent me a link to a lesson I did not reach yet which was Part 2: Are You Ready for Restoration? I realized that I went through my restoration with the same mind. I often felt as though my marriage wasn't restored because my husband didn't feel the need to *work* on our marriage. My expectations were that I expected a complete change from him when he returned. So I'm glad God led the RF Office to send me this link so that I could have a better understanding of what to expect.

Because I tended to focus on the changes my husband wasn't making I completely forgot to praise my heavenly Husband for allowing my husband to return back home when he swore he was getting a divorce. Before this new truth, I found myself regressing back to the old me-- the old me my husband tried so hard to get away from. I even moved to the other ditch where I didn't leave room for my husband to become the spiritual leader because I was trying to do it all! I realized that all of this was due to the enemy turning up the heat on my restored marriage, again, but the Lord knew that I needed to be grounded in Him now more than ever!!! As long as I keep the Lord first in my heart, and He truly is FIRST in my life, it's only then I will begin to see the Lord turn my husband's heart, not only back to me, but more importantly back to Him!!! O PRAISE HIS HOLY AND RIGHTEOUS NAME!!!

Tell us HOW it happened? Did your husband just walk in the front door?

Because I had already been through a restored marriage where it happened unexpectedly, I thought the second time around would be more extravagant. I thought my husband would walk through the door and ask me to take him back. It did not happen this way however. While leaving my door opened, a huge iguana came into my house.

At the time, I was on the phone with my husband (he had called me from work just to hear my voice), when I saw the iguana walk across the floor. I was terrified!!! The next day, after many people tried to remove the iguana, but to no avail, my husband offered to spend the night! That night we were intimate, but I was not sure if this meant our marriage was restored because this had happened before in my first restoration. Still seeking God to determine what this meant, my husband asked me to dinner a couple of days later. During dinner, he told me that he needed me and that he wanted to marry me again! He never said anything like that with my first restoration! It was then that I knew my marriage was restored yet again!!

Did you suspect or could you tell you were close to being restored?

I knew that my marriage was on the verge of restoration, but I just didn't expect it to happen so soon. My main focus was on drawing closer to my heavenly Husband and if my marriage was restored, then that would have been an added bonus. The first time we separated, we were separated for a year, the second time, we were separated for 3 months. So it happened so suddenly, when I least expected it, but because I was following the principles of RMI and spending time with my heavenly Husband, I knew that He would give me the desires of my heart.

Would you recommend any of our resource in particular that helped you?

I recommend completing all of the RRR online courses!!! Pouring out my heart in the "What I Learned" forms helped me to truly make my heavenly Husband my dwelling place. I recommend reading How God can and will Restore your Marriage in its entirety several times! I also recommend the Be Encouraged videos as well as subscribing to the daily Encourager newsletters and submitting praise reports even when you don't feel like it because praise will bind, confuse and break the enemy and cause his hands to be still. These resources helped me to grow as a person and to grow in my relationship with my Lord and Savior.

Would you be interested in helping encourage other women?

I truly feel that God has allowed me to go through this in order to be a blessing the same way RMI has been a blessing to me. I desire to help any and all broken women who feel that their marriage is hopeless through my testimony.

Either way, what kind of encouragement would you like to leave women with in conclusion?

God has the final say on your marriage. No matter how bleak it looks or how hopeless it may seem, it's not over. It's just the beginning. The beginning of a new relationship with your First Love!! Allow God to consume you and let Him be the Leader of your life. Seek Him in all that you do. Do not focus on the whys and why nots but instead focus on loving your heavenly Husband and making Him first and foremost in your life. Then these things will be added unto you. He knows the desires of your heart, so as long as you put your trust in Him, all things will work together for your good.

"Restoration's Temporary Rest"

Only God can give me peace and understanding for what I'm going through and I praise Him that He is allowing me to go through this in order for me to grow! Sadly, I found out my earthly husband found an OW only a month and a half *after* our marriage was restored. He informed me that he no longer wanted to be married to me and would get a divorce if necessary. He decided to remain in the house but said we should remain friends and nothing more. The flesh in me wanted to kick him out but thankfully I remembered my teachings through RMI and God filled me with this verse: 13 "And if a believing woman has a husband who is not a believer and he is willing to continue living with her, she must not leave him.... Don't you wives realize that your husbands might be saved because of you? And don't you husbands realize that your wives might be saved because of you?" (1 Corinthians 7:13, 16 NLT)

Afterwards I went in my car and cried my eyes and heart out to the Lord because I realized I had been backsliding to the old me! "It's better to live alone in the corner of an attic than with a quarrelsome wife in a lovely home". (Proverbs 21:9 NLT) My heavenly Husband has shown me a glimpse of what can happen again if I continue down my old path. Thank You Lord for showing me the error of my ways!!! I will continue to seek You wholeheartedly and be the woman you have called me to be! "In the same way, you wives must accept the authority of your husbands. Then, even if some refuse to obey the Good News, your godly lives will speak to them without any words. They will be won over by observing your pure and reverent lives". (1 Peter 3:1-2 NLT)

God can heal, deliver and mend a broken heart. Once you trust God, He will give you a miracle to fit your needs! No matter what it looks like, and no matter how you feel, never doubt what the Lord is doing in your life because He will work it out and use it for your good! Just trust in God! There is no other way you can make it :)

"Just at the Right Time"

My God has supplied me a miracle to fit my needs just at the right time! When you give it all to your heavenly Husband, and I mean EVERY SINGLE THING, He will move mountains.

In February I filed my taxes and was told that I wouldn't receive my refund until the end of May. When May arrived, I called to find out why I still hadn't received my refund and I was told I needed to refile and it would take an additional 4 months to receive it. Before, I was dependent on receiving this money, but now I put my hope and faith in my heavenly Husband who is my Provider. I gave it all to Him and never gave my refund another thought.

Two weeks later, I scheduled a doctor's appointment because I suffer from a horrible skin condition.This condition has been a nuisance in my life but I already knew that my insurance wouldn't cover the medication I needed. That's when I checked my account to see my balance, I saw my refund check had been deposited!!! PRAISE THE LORD!!! So I was not only able to get my medication, but I also paid to renew my tag had been expired since March.

This, too, came JUST at the right time because I was also offered a new job! Now I don't have to worry about transportation! Lord,

You've been so good to me. I will praise Your Holy Name with every breath that is within me. Thank You Lord! :)

Without RMI, I don't know WHERE my life would be! I thank God for guiding me to this ministry. Honestly, if my Lord did not send me here, I would have continued being the woman I now loathe. I have experienced my Beloved in a whole new light due to this ministry!

Growing up, I was always taught that Jesus is my Lord and Savior. I never knew that He could be my Husband, too, and that He actually WANTED me as His bride!!! I have been refined through the teachings and lessons of RMI, only because they are based solely on the word of God.

Reading the Encourager every morning gives me such joy to see my heavenly Husband working in so many lives! I have found encouragement through the testimonies of such amazing women! These testimonies have even caused me to want my "Sweetheart" the Lord even more! Now, I can't live my life without my Beloved. Tears are streaming down my face now just thinking of His amazing splendor. This is not due to what He has done in my life! This is due to the peace I experienced while living in such a "hopeless" situation. I no longer cried out to others, instead I learn to go to Him for everything!! Now He and I are in constant conversation daily.

It's through RMI that I have learned to depend on Him. This is so new for me because, as I said, I grew up to see Him as my Savior only—to save me when I was in distress. Now I talk to Him about my day, asking Him about His. When I go to bed, I can FEEL His arms wrap around me. I just can't get enough of my amazing Husband. He *is* my Husband!!! He is showing me how a Husband should love His bride and I am truly in awe of how I am being treated by Him, because I never experienced this type of love with anyone else. I am so in love with Him! And it's only due to RMI! Thank you so much!!!

This is why I've applied to become a Minister and be trained through RMIOU because I want to lead others to their Husband!!! Going through a broken marriage is so difficult. Even more difficult if you don't know the One who created marriage! I long to comfort women with the same comfort I received from the Lord.

Even now, daily, I pray to my heavenly Husband to send broken women across my path so that I may be an encouragement to those who are discouraged. While I was in my old church, God has always lead so many individuals my way who have always told me that He wants to use me. Before, I could never understand why or even understand how He would use me. After Him leading me to this ministry, it is now clear :) ~ *Jazmin in Georgia*

Daddy!!!

"And let the wife see to it that
she respect her husband."
—Ephesians 5:33

How did your restoration actually begin?

When I first read the "Are you Ready?" series in my RMI
Encourager, I began to suspect that I already had a restored marriage
but was waiting for what I had imagined my restoration looked like.

As I read the series, I was surprised, because I was not *feeling*
restored, but after reading and Seeking God for wisdom, I then
realized how I was ungrateful... and so, here I am to thank the
Beloved of my soul for everything He has already done and for
everything He has in store for me!

How did your Restoration Journey begin?

My Restoration Journey all started when I realized that my husband
was building a parallel life. I saw that his friends were single men,
and there were always celebrations and "reasons" to go out and arrive
late and drunk.

On the other hand, I started to go out with our children, make new
friends and spend a lot of time with them (and most of the time
drinking, gossiping and badmouthing our husbands!). In addition, I
was faithful to attendance at Sunday Masses, alone or only with my
children.

Despite the serious crisis in our marriage, I decided to plan a family
holiday trip. My husband did not want to travel, but I imagined that it
could be a way to make things get better... I didn't listen to what he
wanted and he stopped to argue, telling me that he would not pay for

the trip, so I told him – showing no respect at all– that I could afford for it!

My husband took us to the hotel, but didn't stay there with us. He told me he had to go back to work and by the weekend he would come to stay with us and take us back home. But he never came and we went home by ourselves.

When we got home, I thought my husband would be waiting for us and at least would be anxious to see the children, but on that day, he arrived late and indifferent! From then on, things only got worse, I found out about the OW and I rubbed it in his face! I felt so lost and confused that I decided to look for a psychologist to help me to become someone different...

I remember that during my visit, I began to enumerate my mistakes and she told me that I could not feel that way and that it was all my husband's fault. She asked me to begin to feel anger and explained me that through anger I would feel free from the guilty I was feeling at that time. Sad and confused, I asked my husband to meet together for us to talk... and so we had the most difficult and painful conversation ever! My husband decided to leave at that day.

How did God change your situation as you sought Him wholeheartedly?

That's when I decided to search on the web for marriages testimonies and when I found Erin's book: "*How God can and will Restore your Marriage*"! PTL!

I began to read it and couldn't stop, and then I read it again and again! I was able to start applying the principles immediately, especially the "letting go". I had to do something - and to have practical advice about how to act, was all I was asking for! I could see the real me, realized my mistakes and understood what was happening! But mainly, I saw that I was not alone and that God had a perfect plan for me! PTL

What principles, from God's Word (or through our resources), did the Lord teach you during this trial?

God began teaching me that I have to hide my heart so deep in Him, making Him always the first One in my life! Letting my husband go, winning without words and having a gentle and quiet spirit was what helped the most.

What were the most difficult times that God helped you through?

The most difficult time that the Lord helped me to go through were with my children, who asked for their father, who were feeling forsaken... I succeeded in not letting them see me crying. I sought God and had help through all the RMIEW materials. So I did not crumble, but stood firm in my faith and remained faithful not only for me, but for them, for our family and future!

What was the "turning point" of your restoration?

The turning point in my situation was immediately when I started applying the principles of "letting go" and "win without words" and of course every other principle I applied, especially having me faithfully continue tithing to my storehouse. But these were the fundamental principles that turned things around, because my husband noticed that I was behaving differently!

One day, after reading about the importance of letting go and asking God to help me truly let him go, my earthly husband sent me a message: *Why don't you call me anymore? What is happening to you?* God is wonderfully faithful to His word and principles!

Tell us HOW it happened? Did your husband just walk in the front door?

Since I began this journey, I've been dreaming of how my restoration would take place: with flowers, new engagement ring, lovely words... then I stopped dreaming of it, and realized it already happened, not in *my* way, but in the best way: in His perfect way for me!

After I found this Ministry (in Portuguese), I began to apply the principles and one day I suddenly heard a noise in the lock of the front door and my husband came into the house! **My children ran to**

him screaming "Daddy!!!!" Even now this scene brings tears to my eyes! I still hear my younger son saying: **"Daddy, you vanished and I missed you so much! Don't do that again please!"** My husband sat down and hugged them with tears in his eyes! He was sad and confused...

In my mind I had a "model" of restoration that I created for myself! Sort of a script in my head with a beginning, middle and an end, but God's plans are not like ours and I know that His plans are much better than mine. So I can only say: May Your will be done in my life Lord!

Thankfully when my husband wasn't at home, I had long and intense days in the presence of my Beloved Jesus! He, through this Ministry, gave me the understanding that I started the Journey of my life and I do not want to return to where and who I was before. After all, where would I go? He alone has the words of eternal life!

Did you suspect or could you tell you were close to being restored?

No, I didn't suspect of anything, I was only trying to be obedient to what I learned, to shut my mouth, to keep my eyes closed (to see not what is seen, but what is unseen) and to allow Him into the person God wants me to be and what He wants me to do!

Would you recommend any of our resource in particular that helped you?

The materials that I recommend are: the book *"How God can and will Restore your Marriage"*— what a blessing of God for us! The book *"A Wise Woman"* that gives practical and specific teachings for a woman who want to be given a spiritual makeover!

I recommend doing the RRR online courses and to read the daily Encourager – so you know how to start the day, I couldn't live without them. And in addition, I recommend writing Praise Reports, pouring your heart out to Jesus in thanks.

Would you be interested in helping encourage other women?

Yes, I am part of the Ministry Team and have been for a while. Now I know there is no greater joy than helping other women! And that God has always had a perfect plan to me, to make me His witness to what He can do for anyone. Now I'm so humbled and so happy because I know that all I've been going through is to help me understand my ministry and I am so excited to share everything He's done for me.

Dear Friend, Jesus, the Beloved of our souls, is eager to be kind to you, to manifest His love and His fondness for you! Among many other women, you have been chosen and will be blessed with the restoration of your marriage, as well as everything He promised and He is faithful! Believe!

~ Andreia in Brazil

Chapter 8

Taken by Surprise!!

"Wait on the Lord,
be of good courage,
yes, wait on the Lord."
—Psalm 27:13

Ava, how did your Restoration Journey begin?

It all began a year ago after I discovered that my husband has an emotional relationship going on with an old girlfriend of his. He admit that he loves her and was convinced that he's in love and that's the person he wants to spend the rest of his life with. He would tell me several times that he doesn't have any feelings for me anymore, he wants us to stay friends for now and wants break from our marriage.

Unfortunately, me being the contentious woman that I was at the time, I called police on my husband and put a restraining order against him soon after I received a phone call from a family member. This family member called to tell me who knew and live in the same state with, which was the other woman. I was also told that the OW already purchase a ticket for my husband to move in with her in Florida before the weekend.

That same day before I received the phone call I heard my husband talking with the OW about how happy and excited he was and how he couldn't wait. That's when I made my next big mistake because I started to panic and began calling all my friends and family members about the situation.

My husband told me he got invited to a party in New York that night and *might* come back home the next day if he didn't find a train running. Yet I didn't buy it and call cops on him while he was taking a shower as suggested by some family members and friends and I told the cops that he put his hands on me. They arrested him for a few hours and ask him to find a place to stay because I requested a restraining order.

That night my husband went to New York and stayed with a friend but I felt so bad for putting him through all this that I contacted him asking for his forgiveness. He said he forgave me but he would never forget, and said he would *never* in his put his feet in my house again. It's at that low point when I started to seek God for forgiveness and began to search for real help. And that's when the Lord lead me to this ministry.

How did God change your situation as you sought Him wholeheartedly?

God showed me all my wrong doings and I was able to forgive myself for what I'd done and my husband as well. My whole life and situation began to change when God introduced me to His Son, my Lord who became my heavenly Husband. He opened my eyes, gave me a new heart and lead me to the truth. I remember there was times I wouldn't hear from my husband for months; but the closer I got to the Lord, the more He'd prompt my husband to call and soon the hate wall fell. The Lord change *everything* around for better!

What principles, from God's Word (or through our resources), did the Lord teach you during this trial?

During this trial, I learned that the most important principle is to put my Lord Jesus Christ first in everything I do! He should have the first place in my life all along: not my husband, not my job or anything else. It's when I put Him first that I began seeing His mercy. I also learned to wait on the lord and let His will be done rather than rush the process. Another thing I learned is that no matter what the trial may be— don't fright—and rejoice always.

What were the most difficult times that God helped you through?

The most difficult time was seeing my husband falling in love with another woman. I was really hurt by that; but, the Lord kept on reminding me that He's the one in control and I should trust Him because he will not put me to shame.

Another difficult time was financial issue when I was at a point when I could no longer support myself nor pay my rent. But through that difficulty I learned that He faithfully provides for all my needs once that I began tithing and trusting in Him for everything.

What was the "turning point" of your restoration?

The turning point of my restoration is honestly when the Lord lead me to this awesome ministry. I was a dead spirit then, but all glory to the Lord— He uses Erin and this ministry to show me the way! It wasn't until I truly met my Lord and His Word became my everything that I began seeing tremendous transformations in my life.

Tell us HOW your Restoration happened?

My husband did not just walk in the front door. First, he'd been reduced to bread of loaf as said and began going through some really difficult times. He had been unemployed for months and simply couldn't take it anymore. He had been telling me how he couldn't find a job no matter how hard he tried.

Then one day he called to ask me if my job was hiring. I said yes, so he applied online, then got an interview with them but never showed up. The reason he gave me was that he couldn't see himself living in New Jersey because of how he hate it there and could never live there again. And based on what I learned, I never asked him to come live here and instead all I said was OK.

It was on the first of January when he called to say Happy New Year but began complaining about me not calling him and we didn't speak to each other if he wasn't the one to call. That's when I mentioned that it was because I'd been busy moving in to my new apartment. Three days later around 6pm he called to tell me that he'd just gotten kicked out of where he was living and needed my help. He asked me if he could come home because he didn't have anyone else but me. I was honestly shocked because I didn't know my restoration was gonna happened that way. Yes, the Lord took me by surprise but I trust Him.

For the past 2 weeks I continue telling the Lord how He's all I need and how I don't even care about my marriage anymore because He's given me everything I need and because I'm so happy where I'm at right now in my life with Him. I was actually pleading with Him not to let my husband come back (before he called) because I've been enjoying the peace with Him. I've even told one of my closest friends the same thing.

So I confess I was sad when my husband asked me if he could come home because I've been enjoying the peace I get with my Lord. I did thank the Lord for what He's done, answered the prayer I'd prayed, but at the same time, I was honestly sad.

Praise the Lord. My husband has been home for 2 weeks now and he reapplied for the same job, got an interview and got the job. Now he's just waiting for his schedule. Again, Praise the Lord!

As for our relationship, at this point we're just like friends. We don't have the normal husband and with relationship, not yet. Nothing major has change yet, but I know my Lord is still working to change us both.

Did you suspect or could you tell you were close to being restored?

Yes, I knew I was close to being restored because almost everybody who knew about my situation began agreeing in prayer for my restoration and would tell me to get ready without me mentioning *anything* to anyone.

The main key I learned about restoration is that it happens when you don't need it and honestly don't want it.

Would you recommend any of our resource in particular that helped you?

Yes, I would recommend the "how God can and will restore your marriage" book, the bible, along all the videos and courses.

The daily Encouragers helped me a lot also because they kept me motivated to gain the relationship with the Lord that I was lacking. In addition I always make sure I go back to the videos whenever I need a boost of encouragement.

What kind of encouragement would you like to leave women with in conclusion?

I'd like to encourage you ladies to never give up no matter what your situation may look like, no matter what you've been told, and no matter what has happened. Keep your faith in God alone and know that He's more able to do the impossible.

Finally, be sure to Wait on the Lord.

~ Ava in New York

Chapter 9

I'm Ready to Move Back Home

"With people this is impossible,
but with God all things are possible."
—Matthew 19:26

Daniela, how did your restoration actually begin?

I had experienced depression for as long as I could remember, but I didn't become truly aware of this until after my son was born and I received a diagnosis. With the diagnosis came multiple types of medications. The side-effects included exhaustion, brain fog, weight gain and anger issues and combined these effects had a tremendous impact on my relationship with my hb. Just before our 10th wedding anniversary, I had made a huge decision without informing my hb and it was the 'straw that broke the camels back'. I didn't know until later that someone had been sowing into his life for nearly two years and planting seeds for him to leave me. We made the decision to separate in July, 2010. He left in September and by November, I was crying out to God for answers.

How did God change your situation as you sought Him wholeheartedly?

One night, after trying to figure out why I felt so strongly about the 'vow' I made and couldn't let go of our marriage, I was asking God, "why?" My heart felt like it had literally been torn in two. I sat at my dining room table with my laptop in front of me when all of a sudden, as I cried out to God in anguish, I saw an image of him with the cross on his back and he had fallen to the ground. It was almost as though He was giving me a tiny glimpse into a pain that only He could endure. I reached out and began to type on the keyboard - I cannot recall what I typed, I was so distressed. The next thing I knew, I was opening a facebook page that provided resources and information about restoration! I didn't even know that restoration was an option for me and I had been a Christian for most of my life!!! As soon as I went on to the site a lady began talking with me. She had just finished asking God to send her someone who was desperate for Him. And there I was!!! She began to share with me about Erin Thiele's from Restore Ministries and the realities of 'standing' for my marriage.

What principles, from God's Word (or through our resources), did the Lord teach you during this trial?

One of the most important realities for me was the fact that with God, nothing is impossible. I had a child-like faith for some things but I didn't know how to ask and that was another key area of learning for me - "You do not have because you do not ask." The realities of making significant changes in my life and removing the outlandish expectations I had placed on my hb were life-changing. I followed God's Word, not man's. It was difficult to do but I knew without a shadow of a doubt that God was doing something amazing.

What were the most difficult times that God helped you through?

I was so tormented about the idea of my hb possibly finding someone else. This just about destroyed me. I knew the enemy was putting people in his path but I believed in God's word: "They shall come out against you one way and flee before you seven ways." Deut 28:7. I would also pray the hedge of thorns around my family asking God to prevent evil from coming near us, and that the heart of my hb would be for the wife of his youth. It was amazing to watch as God moved to protect us!!!

What was the "turning point" of your restoration?

There were times when I would be so tormented. If I hadn't heard from hb for a few days, fear would try to take a hold of me. BUT GOD!!! I relied on the scriptures that were so relevant, so true, as torches that shone in those darkest, scariest moments of my life! My hb was tempted. I know this. But I can tell you I was AMAZED to watch as I believe God sent one lady to another country! A man who had been sowing seeds of destruction and worked with my hb retired and NOT ONCE has he crossed the threshold of our home - which I prayed and believed in God to prevent! Another woman who worked with my hb had been relying on him emotionally and I believe God caused her to take another job that forced her to travel so much, they lost complete contact!!! Praise GOD!!!! Indeed, watching all of this unfold, were all instrumental to bringing my hb back home to us.

Tell us HOW it happened? Did your husband just walk in the front door?

After my husband left, I rented out our five bedroom home and moved into a smaller house with two bedrooms for myself and our son. The house had issues with mold and moisture that made me quite ill. I had to send my son to be with his father because I was fearful that he would become sick. It was around this time that my hb bought a house, for the purpose of a place for me and my son to live. It was truly amazing. One of the major issues in our marriage was the fact that I was bitter about the responsibilities that came with higher income. I believe God allowed great healing to take place as my hb was given his rightful authority in these areas. It was because the house was his that he felt comfortable enough to drop by. I didn't push or pursue or place any restrictions on him - I just prayed and left it in God's hands. My hb would mention things along the way that gave me an impression that he wanted to come home, but I never felt released to mention this to him. Instead, I asked God to use my words and was very, very careful with what I would say. I will never forget the evening when he had dropped by. He was standing at the kitchen counter and I had just come out of the laundry room in the hallway. I looked at him and and he turned around and said, "I think I'm ready to move back home, now."

Did you suspect or could you tell you were close to being restored?

I had been asking God to restore my hb to Him first, before allowing him to come back home. I truly had left it all in God's hands and did everything in my power to avoid manipulating or trying to coerce the situation. In retrospect, I think I was at a point where I had simply gone through every painful event that could possibly have occurred and my faith had been stretched to a point that I was just at a place of 'peace'. For the entire time of this journey, I felt close to restoration. There were times of great stress and doubt, absolutely, but once I agreed with God, I felt it would happen at any time.

Would you recommend any of our resource in particular that helped you?

I gained such healing from the "*How God CAN and WILL Restore your Marriage.*" resource! Also, the "*Wise Women*" resources have been instrumental - not only for me but for many of my friends as well. We have seen healing restorations take place, I believe firmly, because of the teachings in these resources.

Would you be interested in helping encourage other women?

Oh, yes!

Either way, what kind of encouragement would you like to leave women with in conclusion?

Nothing - absolutely NOTHING - is impossible with God. He loves us with an everlasting love and when we have faith and make our petitions known to God, when we take the time and learn HIS message for us, the mountains WILL move! Only believe and receive!!

~ *Daniella in Canada*

Chapter 10

Rewarded for my Obedience & Love for Him

"Why do you call Me,
'Lord, Lord,'
and do not do what I say?"
—Luke 6:46

My journey started in September when my life was crumbling and full of hopelessness. Back in July I found out my husband was committing adultery for the second time, then told me he was leaving and ask for divorce. God talked to me in a dream that night and told me to start praying for my husband, but I was so full of despair that no word would come out of my mouth. I found a book that I had about praying and started reading the prayers for my husband everyday. I was desperate and began seeking help in every way possible to save my marriage when I found a reference in Facebook to RYM book Spanish version. I download it and started reading. By the time I got to chapter 3 I was in tears—knowing deep in my heart that was God talking to me through this book.

How did God change your situation as you sought Him wholeheartedly?

By the time I finished reading RYM book I put my life and my situation in God's hands. I have never read the Bible, so I bought one and started looking up every verse and chapter mentioned in the book. I wrote out all the verses on 3x5 cards. Immediately I was longing to read more and my heavenly Husband started to speak to me. I started to have peace and a lot of things started to change for good inside me and around me.

What principles, from God's Word (or through our resources), did the Lord teach you during this trial?

His promise was given to me and every word was a confirmation that I was on the right track. I choose the narrow road and stay still like my heavenly Husband told me to. I also fully let go of my earthly husband, which was the hardest thing to do, but my heavenly Husband was there all the time to keep me safe and helped me feel loved.

What were the most difficult times that God helped you through?

My earthly husband had been in adultery since June, then left the house in October to share an apartment with a co worker. In December he filed for divorce and the court papers arrived at my door in December while my neighbors were helping me put up my front garden and our children were playing in the street. I gathered my strength in my heavenly Husband and took the papers inside. I went to my prayer closet, into the arms of my heavenly Husband and in pain and sorrow I asked for success, but knowing in my heart that divorce *was* part of His plan and I needed to be obedient and stay still.

My Lord was so gracious, during that next week and He gave me blessings that I could never imagine I would have in my entire life. The blessing was Him showing me His love in so many ways as a reward for my obedience and love for Him. In January, I went to court for the mandatory child support hearing. I did exactly what Erin suggested in the RYM and went with the best lawyer ever, Jesus, and who is the judge of all judges and my almighty God! PTL!

Yes, I was nervous, but He was there carrying me all through the hearing.

In March we had the second hearing in court and divorce was a final that day. This time I was less nervous and even more full of strength at the hearing (praying and praising the Lord in silence all the time) until the last word was said. Running to my prayer closet was not possible at the time, so I went to sit quietly at on the oceanfront near my workplace to cry myself out with my heavenly Husband. After that I notice that every time I fell on my knees for my situations I was able to stand back up faster and firmly on my feet only by His Grace.

What was the "turning point" of your restoration?

Time flew and situations with my earthly husband and the OW started to happen, but my heavenly Husband was so gracious and loving with me that I could go through them in peaceful ways and full of contentment. This does not mean that I didn't got mad at times, but I remembered that I needed to be "slow to anger and plenteous in mercy" Psalm 103: 8.

By September my earthly husband moved in with the OW and hardship was striking even with my two boys; they didn't cope well with the situation and it was hard for them to stay with their father.

Tell us HOW it happened? Did your husband just walk in the front door?

Things were happening so fast. My earthly husband bought a car for the OW in September and a engagement ring early in November for her birthday. I was surprised but at the same time in perfect peace. My feelings of letting go was clearly complete. I was living and doing everything how God wanted me to, with some flaws now and then, but with peace in my heart because my heavenly Husband walks with me all the time.

Then suddenly in December at 3:20pm I received a text message from my earthly husband that read like this:

"I don't know why I'm telling you this but I want my family back, let God do his will. I don't Know what is going to happen from now on but I feel in my heart that I need to tell you this."

I was walking to my classroom to gather my things, so I hurriedly closed the door and fell on my knees praising, praying and thanking my heavenly Husband for His goodness and fulfilling His will on me and my family.

We saw each other that evening, my earthly husband talked his heart out and in tears told me that he wanted God in his life. PTL! He ask for forgiveness and if I wanted him in my life again. I told him that I forgave him long time ago, and if I needed to, I'd choose him as a husband.

We established a plan that began for the next few days: to come and pray together so every plan moving forward was God's will and purpose first before anything we wanted. The next day he gathered his things and in the afternoon we went to dinner with our two boys and gave them the good news. I will never forget the look and the smiles of my two sons that day. My earthly husband asked them for forgiveness in tears and the only thing that they could do was hug him very hard. He moved in to our guest-room and we continued working our restoration the best that we can with God as our guide.

Did you suspect or could you tell you were close to being restored?

I did not suspect at all that I was so close. I actually thought that it was going to take more time but was fine since I had my heavenly Husband.

Would you recommend any of our resource in particular that helped you?

I recommend RYM book, *A Wise Woman*, all of Erin's videos, *Word of the testimony*, RYM Questions and answers, *My Beloved*, Encourager, The Praise Report.

Would you be interested in helping encourage other women?

Yes, I would like to encouraged other women in my country and in my first language Spanish.

What kind of encouragement would you like to leave women with in conclusion?

Beloved I encouraged you to keep your faith, believe,pray, praise, be still and let your heavenly Husband do his job. He loves you and Knows what's best for you. He wants you to be a renew woman in Him so you can receive what he promise. He is a God of word and you will see his grace and mercy! PTL!

~ Myrnaliz in Puerto Rico

Chapter 11

Husband Suddenly Came Home Broken

"He who began the good work within you,
will continue His work until it is finally finished
on the day when Christ Jesus returns."
— Philippians 1:6

It all began when my earthly husband left in January 2013 after 2 months of squabbling and painful exchanges. When he left, I felt like a rug was pulled out from under me because I was caught by surprise! I never suspected that there might have been someone else because I trusted my earthly husband a lot and I thought we had a really great marriage, quite honestly. Little did I know that with my earthly husband it was a totally different story.

My husband had been harboring ill feelings towards me for the past 14 years while being married, explaining that I never valued him, that he felt controlled and emotionally abused, that he no longer loved me and that he felt our marriage was hopeless! When he told me, I confess, I responded quite angrily especially when he started coming home at sunrise, drunk and disrespectful. I threw a fit and because I was so mad, I left our home and went straight to a friend's house. I poured out all my anger towards him to all my friends and I said I would not go home and speak to him if he did not try to fix the mess "he" started. This ultimatum pushed him to decide to leave the house and our family.

The first few months were horrible. I went into a deep depression. So I ran to every single person I knew to get help and everyone had a different version of help to give to me—ranging from seducing him back to me to filing for my annulment. During this time I lost 15 pounds and was a measly 99 lbs. in weight! It took me several month of craziness in my life (by crazy I mean I would go out drinking with my friends, stalking facebook and his friends, reading all kinds of books and websites about marriage and winning a guy back) before I found RMI. The breaking point was after 8 months of being separated when it was finally confirmed that there was an OW was involved. That's when I asked God to show me, to help to know how to deal with this situation because I just literally wanted to die already and be over with the pain. That's when I typed in "Does God want to restore my marriage?" and I found your site!!

That's when the Lord began to change me and deal with me, primarily, on the area of control. He brought me to so many situations where He needed to show me were not possible if not for Him. He also allowed me to see how badly the turnout would be when I pursued being in control of a situation, which made me surrender (several times because it was too hard) so my will would be to follow His.

The principles that God, through RMI, taught me were:

1) **Putting God first**. In my entire married life, I put everything or everyone **first** before God. I would think the number one thing in my life was myself. I put my needs before God, my husband and my kids.

2) **Removing contention and keeping quiet**. For someone who wants to be in control of situations, *contention* is not too far away from a *conversation*. Throughout this entire trial, God showed me that a lot of what pushed my earthly husband to leave me had to do with my need to get my way and not let go of an argument! I believe this is something we don't learn in just one go... it's still a process for me now, so God is still dealing with me on this. When I am humbled in the presence of the Lord, especially when I've spend time in prayer, it is easy to be gentle and kind and quiet in my earthly husband's presence. But when I am tired and I allow anger and pride to return, I need to be careful to still keep my mouth shut when needed.

3) **Seeking God**. I grew up an only child where my parents were almost never home, and so I always had the need to talk to someone and feel validated by a person. Throughout this last year, the Lord removed several people from my life so He could lead me to seek Him for questions that I needed answers or decisions that were to be made. And to be validated by Him.

Some of the hardest times for me were when I knew there was an OW, but that's when the Lord kept filling me with grace and unconditional love for my earthly husband. God gave me a daily double dose of His grace to forgive my earthly husband and the OW and to pray for them both even when my hurt was unbelievably deep!

The turning point of my restoration was when I was invited to a prayer group and was asked to share to the attendees how God helped me through the storms in my life. I was able to talk about how God was amazing in taking care of me and the kids, how He became a Heavenly Husband to me and how He assured me that no matter what, He will never leave me or forsake me.

Immediately after this one afternoon activity, I felt an onslaught of the enemy's attacks on me. I was feeling all sorts of anxiety and doubts about my journey. I was questioning whether I had done the right thing, if I should have just kept quiet about the Lord's workings in my life, if I should just give up, etc.

Then 2 weeks prior to my earthly husband's return, God led me to start reading several chapters of the Bible, in the book of Numbers, which talked about how the Israelites' complainings had angered the Lord so much, that He caused them to wander 40 more years in the desert. I clearly recalled repenting for any complaining that I might have been doing and crying to Him that I was more than content with my situation at present, with Him taking care of all our needs and being in control of my life. Yet I definitely did not want to wander the desert of my life for 40 years! A week before earthly husband's return, God then told me to read Deuteronomy 6:10 all the way until Deuteronomy 8. I was wondering the whole time, "Was the Lord bringing me already into my promised land?" Because it surely didn't look anything like it. I poured over these verses and wrote in my journal everything that the Lord spoke to me.

Then, suddenly one morning, I woke up to the sound of my doorbell ringing. Thinking it was the carpenter who was to do repairs, I went to the door to see my earthly husband standing in my living room, looking tired, dressed in clothes he seemed to have slept in. He asked me if he could use my bathroom and if he could leave his car at my garage as he was planning to go home to my in-laws and just have them pick him up. I asked him if he was alright because I got worried that he looked so distraught. He held my arm and simply said "Please just keep praying for me" when I got even more concerned. So I asked him if there was anything he needed my help with. That's when a tear broke from his eye and he said he was ok. That night he slept for the first time in our house and was in and out for several weeks before he finally making the decision to stay.

In a span of a week, I was told by a common friend that my earthly husband and the OW were no longer together for a few months already, and that he was going through depression for not having a job for more than a year. He was down to nothing...no work, no money, no OW, no home! My earthly husband moved back home suddenly!! Unlike what I expected in the testimonies I've read in the past (a few I read in *By Word of Their Testimony* book) and heard from friends whose marriages were restored, my husband did not come home crying and asking for *my* forgiveness. He actually returned home broken, coming back quietly and expressed a desire to fix his life with his kids primarily, and to try to fix his family relationship, but is not ready to deal with our marriage yet. Nevertheless I know He will finish what He started and give me more time to be more of a wise woman.

For women who are interested in restoring their marriages, I would highly recommend the *How God Can and Will Restore Your Marriage* book. I have actually recommended it to several women already who I know are going through a crisis in their marriages. I have also shared this site to a few women for them to explore on their own :).

Just like all of you, I was very scared of this journey I found myself in. To completely let go of control over our life and our circumstances can be the scariest thing to do everyday especially if you were like me who always thought they had everything under control and figured out. But to know a loving Father, a faithful Heavenly Husband, a Confidante, and a Best Friend the way God has been to me, as well as to have a much deeper relationship with His Son Jesus is one of the most fulfilling experiences you can ever have during this whole process. It may not "feel" like anything good is happening nor does it "look" like things will change, but to really just walk each day by faith believing what God has promised you, you will see the breakthroughs a bit at a time to get you till the end of this journey!

Since my earthly husband came back home a month ago, my heavenly Husband has been showing me small victories every day of giving me the desires of my heart. So far my heavenly Husband has restored me to my in-laws (I have been included in family gatherings again after almost 2 years if not seeing them), and He has granted my need for dental work (my earthly husband brought me and our kids for dental checks) so everything will be free of charge! Also after almost 2 years, my family started going back to church together with our spiritual leader.

I know my full and completed restoration is within sight, this is going to be a slow process still as I can clearly see how God is still needing to change me and how He is working in my earthly husband's life. Sometimes I become frightened over the thought that since we really haven't spoken about *reconciliation* yet, so that anytime my earthly husband can just change his mind and leave. But unlike in the past, I have a confidence in a God, a heavenly Husband who is in control of my life and my marriage. I know that as God works through me, He will continue to soften my earthly husband's heart and turn it back fully to Him and then to me.

"And I am certain that God, who began the good work within you, will continue His work until it is finally finished on the day when Christ Jesus returns." Phil 1:6

Whatever happens I am secure in the love of my heavenly Husband who promises to never ever leave me nor forsake me! And this love is ALL that I truly need and truly want and live for! Praise God, my Heavenly Husband!

~Peachy in Philippines

Husband Gives Wife
our RYM Book

"Cleansing her
with the washing of water
by the word"
— Ephesians 5:26

Ministry Note: The testimony you are about to read is different than most, because it was Jodi's husband who found RMI and began following the principles. Unlike a woman, a man can share things as her spiritual leader, if asked, like him sharing the RYM book with her. Hopefully you will be able to glean many wonderful insights, without making the mistake of doing things that are reserved for men seeking restoration.

I am a born-again Christian. In the Lord's mercy for me, He saved me from my life riddled with drugs, alcohol, and crime for the sake of myself and my three beautiful children. I have been clean and sober for many years, all praises to God. However, I still had a lot of issues I was trying to heal from, which affected my marriage. My husband and I are of different cultures. We had a tumultuous relationship filled with anger, resentment, and bitterness. We fought and argued constantly. Neither I nor my husband felt any peace in our home. My husband didn't feel loved by me, so he turned to other options. One day I discovered that he was surfing the web looking for other women and on dating sites. I was devastated, but continued to remain faithful to him hoping that things would change.

Things did change in our marriage – for the worse, and eventually we separated. I remained intimate with my husband during our separation, but soon discovered that he was also sinking deeper into sin. When I found out, I wanted to die. I made the mistake of uncovering my husband's nakedness to everyone I knew including my church. I sought counseling from my church, who advised me to move on with my life.

Although I did plan to move on with my life, I believed my husband was the one for life – until death do us part, yet my feelings of hate for him were very strong. As God tells us in His Word "Let all bitterness, anger and clamor and evil speaking be put away with malice." (Ephesians 4:31 NIV). I was not able to put my bitterness away and allow God to heal and work within me. Although conflicted, I still began divorce proceedings, happily to get rid of my husband. I even cut myself free from him, mentally, during one of my church's prayer meetings. There was no way that I was going to continue to be married to someone who I thought was the devil.

While I believed my husband was the devil, the Lord was changing him for the better. My husband began fasting and praying for our marriage, and eventually became a member of the Encouraging Men website. He confessed to me one day that he was standing for our marriage. He even gave me a copy of *How God Can and Will Restore Your Marriage!* I thought, how bold was he and how dare he! I was livid, and told him not to bother praying for such a crazy thing, as it wasn't going to happen. A few weeks after my husband revealed this to me, I found myself deep in worship at a woman's revival conference, and having the Word and testimonies of others poured into me. It was at this conference that God spoke to my heart saying 'I can even fix your marriage.' I was devastated. I couldn't understand why God would want me back with my husband after the way he treated and disrespected me. I shared this revelation with some trusted friends, and my pastors. My pastors were furious. They even drove to my house to tell me that what I heard was not of God. They never once advised me to SG in my marriage situation. These were supposed to be men of God! I didn't know what to do, and grew more confused. I felt alone and empty inside, and often had suicidal thoughts.

Rather than seeking God for the answers and to fill my void, I turned to another man, and became involved in an adulterous relationship. I knew I was in disobedience to God, but stayed in the relationship. This relationship did not fill the void that I had; it only made me feel worse. I felt like dying, and to make matters worse, I became pregnant by the other man (OM). My pastors were informed and were mortified. They disowned me, and wanted nothing to do with me. However, I still remained in the relationship. All the while, God was using this awful situation for good, and began convicting the OM.

God showed the OM in a dream that I still loved my husband, and that He was going to restore both our marriages. When the OM shared this with me, I cried out to the Lord and then to my husband. My husband was not only forgiving, but he also promised to be a good father for the baby. We began talking more and spending time together. When I became sick a few weeks later, the OM disappeared, but it was my husband who stood by me taking me to my doctor's appointments. Shortly afterwards, I began bleeding and had to have emergency surgery for an ectopic pregnancy. It was a painful reminder of my sins. When everyone else abandoned me, the Lord allowed my husband to stay by my side, taking me to the hospital for the surgery and taking care of me after it. My husband was not the devil I remembered him to be, but a Godly man. My husband was constantly talking about God and bible scriptures, and even listening to Christian music. Before this time, he hated listening to my Christian music! Proverbs 21:1 tells us that "the king's heart is like channels of water in the Lord's hand; He turns it wherever He wishes". I was seeing this verse come to pass firsthand. My husband had changed so much, which was only the work of God!

It was the changing of my husband that God used to soften my heart. As my heart continued to soften, my husband and I grew closer together, and to Christ. We ultimately reconciled and began living for Christ as the center of our lives. We recently renewed our wedding vows. Everyone thought I was crazy for taking my husband back. My pastors are completely against it, and were more concerned with the image of their church than for the salvation of me and my husband or what was best for our family. They saw me as a distraction and completely disowned me. It was through God's grace and mercy alone, however that saved me and restored my marriage. When I couldn't let go of the images of my husband sinning, God stepped in and helped me. No one else has the power to do such things - not pastors, husband, family or friends. Not even me. All those times I cried out to God and prayed for Him to make my husband a Godly man on fire for Him did not go unheard.

I thank God for His mercy and grace. I thank God for using my husband to bring me to this ministry, and for giving me the RYM book. When I came here and filled out a Marriage Evaluation, I hadn't read it. It took just a month from filling out the evaluation until I filled out this restored marriage testimony. I have already recommended the ministry's resources to my friends because of how quickly they worked and helped me. One friend in particular just received the final divorce papers. So I am helping her navigate through RMI's website and encouraging her. I am believing for her marriage to be restored too, even though the divorce went through. God is a God of restoration. Only He can fix it!

Don't give up my friends! I am believing with you that God is going to perform a miracle in your situation. Draw near to Him just as I am learning to do. It is a process, but only God can heal and restore. God loves each one of you and cares for you so much. He doesn't want to see us sorrowful and desires for us to have an intimate relationship with Him. Two of my favorite Bible verses that God gave to me are Psalm 56:8: (NKJV) "You number my wanderings and collect my tears in a bottle. Are they not in Your book?" and Psalm 126:5-6 (NKJV) "Those who sow in tears shall reap joy in the morning. He who continually goes forth weeping, bearing seed for sowing shall doubtless come again rejoicing bringing his sheaves with him." All the sowing through the tears, hurt and pain you have and are suffering will be rewarded if you just seek God first. No my dear sisters, God has not forgotten about you. Cry out to Him in your darkest hour. Offer up sacrificial praises unto Him. Spend time with Him in your joyful moments, as well. He is waiting for you!

~Jodi in Australia

Our next chapter is Jodi's husband's Testimony submitted a few months later.

Chapter 13

Hostility until the
DAY of
My Breakthrough!

"Wait on the Lord,
be of good courage,
yes, wait on the Lord."
— Psalm 27:13

Failure of my marriage was sealed when I continued to have a secret and habitual sin of pornography. This eventually led to me being adulterous. I was always too proud to seek God to help me, even when my wife confronted me. I shifted the blame from myself and denied it every time I was caught.

The first time I sought help from a Christian counselor, my wife and I were going through a divorce. The Christian counselor told me that God had allowed me to be exposed not to destroy my marriage, but to restore it and to save my life. After our conversation I went online, typed "restored marriages" into a search engine, and found Restore Ministries (RMI). It was very confronting to confess what I had done when I filled out my forms. However, I was so tired of cover-ups and lies that I confessed. I wanted to change. I received my marriage evaluation back from RMI, which really lifted my spirit. The RMI books were very difficult to accept because I saw my failures even more clearly with every page.

Yet that's when God began changing me. I got into my bible like I had never before in my life. I started to pray twice a day for about 30 minutes, and just praising God before my prayers. I sang my favourite hymns and found myself listening to nothing but Praise, Worship and Gospel music. I started making immediate changes, and found a new church and bible study group. I became so changed that even I could not believe it was me anymore! I received even more help from a Christian ministry in dealing with my desire to look at porn. I didn't stop there; I kept going. I got amazing support at my new church. God is so amazing because only He could have directed me to this church. God became my sunrise and sunset.

During my trials, God taught me two big lessons; having faith and staying consecrated. So many people, even close friends and family, told me to give up, move on, and find another girlfriend. I told one friend that I was standing for my marriage and he called me "delusional". All through this my wife continued to be really hostile towards me. There were no signs of progress at all. It seemed as if there was a large army assembled against my marriage being restored, but I kept praying and making changes. In the midst of all of this, I learned to keep thinking "But God is greater than all these things" and to carry the word of God in my heart for all these situations

The most difficult times that God helped me through was dealing with my wife. Sometimes, as if my wife was not hostile enough, she would be even more "over the top hostile". Her words crushed me. I sometimes felt that my wife would make seeing our children really hard for me. I kept turning the other cheek and remembering that Jesus stood falsely accused by the Pharisees in front of Pilate yet said nothing. His Love kept silent. So I stayed silent.

Because of my wife's hostility towards me, I did not suspect that my restoration was close. There were no signs of marriage restoration until the very end. In fact, the opposite was true. Dealings with my wife got worse for me and it seemed that she became even more hostile. She kept confessing how much hatred she had for me and how much we would "never ever" be together. Her friend, at the time, from her church was only too happy to serve me with divorce papers.

I continued to pray even *after* I *signed* divorce papers. I did everything in faith and trusted that the divorce would not pass. I planned to have "marriage restoration party" and did not plan how we would split the little we had. I was living with non-Christian roommates at the time, and they openly confessed that they thought I had "cracked".

Suddenly, out of the blue, my wife asked how to restore a marriage when I was picking up the children one Sunday morning. I told her a bit of what I read about in the RMI books and other resources I had been using. She was skeptical, but the hostility ended that very day. She called me the next day and we started spending time together again. My wife just started speaking to me suddenly. At that point; picking up and dropping off children had descended into a " wordless transaction" but from that day we spoke, the phone calls became more frequent, and she started asking me to her house for dinner in order to spend time with her and help her with the children.

At this point, I am interested in helping to encourage other men, and encourage them to never stop seeking the Lord. Please don't ever stop praying, worshipping or seeking the Lord in His word. Because I stopped and fell back into adultery, I now watch out for that devil who is roaring and looking for prey . My wife and I are still together, and we have more community at church to help us get better at our marriage.

My men's bible study group, which I still attend, carried me and prayed with me during that time. I have podcasts in the car and have just replaced all my secular habits with Godly ones. So, don't let your guard down for a moment, and have a men's Christian community even when your marriage is restored.

Dear friend and for all the men reading my testimony I want to encourage you and praise the Lord because He was worked in my life by restoring my marriage and now I pleased that I can help and ministering to other men.

I am glad you've found this book and hope you've been taking advantage of the resources RMI provides for free. If you are seeking restoration, what is most important right now is that you grow in your relationship with the Lord.

As I've said through my testimony is that Jesus has saved me, not only has He worked in my life (and later in my wife's life), but also by restoring our marriage and through this same power by resurrecting it. Most importantly, He has worked in my own personal restoration. Jesus has brought me out of the habitual sin (addiction if you like) of pornography, adultery, luke warmness, secrecy, deceit, wrong thinking and pride.

If I could say one thing about my marriage, which led up to getting divorced, is that I was a complete fool. I was completely ignorant of what it meant to be a husband and father. I professed Christianity but I had very little of the fruit. I had been married for four years and it had ended up in a disaster. It's only when I sat in the rubble (of my marriage), with my life that seemed to be like a building that had been bombed, that I was able to see my error.

The first time I opened a Bible to read something on marriage was when I was going through my divorce. I had been separated for ten of the twelve months that were necessary for my wife to apply for a divorce in Western Australia. It was then that in brokenness and desperation that I took the Word of the Lord and my Bible seriously.

2 Timothy 3:16-17 "All Scripture is God-breathed and is useful for teaching, rebuking, correcting and training in righteousness, so that the servant of God may be thoroughly equipped for every good work."

I started to look up what the Lord expected of a Husband and every chapter that I looked up in the Bible completely pointed a finger at all my failures. I had failed on every account and it was shocking to me. I had failed because in the four years that I had been married, I had never sought the Lord seriously. I had stayed in a marriage for four years without the wisdom and the power of the Word of the Lord.

It was also then that I found out that all of my ideas and expectations about marriage, my faith, what I thought was Christianity and the Word of the Lord were either distorted, misguided—plainly wrong or vague at best. While I was married, the word of God, through the Bible, had never been thought about, meditated upon, or seriously prayed about, or followed by me – Ever!

Psalm 119:9-16 "How can a young person stay on the path of purity? By living according to your word. I seek you with all my heart; do not let me stray from your commands. I have hidden your word in my heart that I might not sin against you. Praise be to you, Lord; teach me your decrees."

"With my lips I recount all the laws that come from your mouth. I rejoice in following your statutes as one rejoices in great riches. I meditate on your precepts and consider your ways. I delight in your decrees; I will not neglect your word."

In addition, following counsel from another Christian at this time, I joined a new Church and this confrontation of my failure went on even further to completely expose more of my foolishness.

The first few sermons I attended at this new church were about the sin of pornography/lust and how the word of God was needed in marriages. It was really hard to sit in that church and get more confronted about my sin. But I knew I had to "stick it out" this time as I had just had enough of blame shifting and not dealing with my failures/sins in the past. I just could not go back to that sinful lifestyle. After all, what had I gained by a sinful and foolish lifestyle? - Nothing! What had I lost? -Everything!

Psalm 119:25-31 "I am laid low in the dust; preserve my life according to your word. I gave an account of my ways and you answered me; teach me your decrees. Cause me to understand the way of your precepts, that I may meditate on your wonderful deeds. My soul is weary with sorrow; strengthen me according to your word."

Psalm 119:37-40 "Keep me from deceitful ways; be gracious to me and teach me your law. I have chosen the way of faithfulness; I have set my heart on your laws. I hold fast to your statutes, Lord; do not let me be put to shame. Turn my eyes away from worthless things; preserve my life according to your word. Fulfill your promise to your servant so that you may be feared. Take away the disgrace I dread, for your laws are good. How I long for your precepts! In your righteousness preserve my life. Remember your word to your servant, for you have given me hope."

I started to attend one of the men's groups in church, primarily to pray and to read the Word of God daily. While you are alone, be sure to use this time has been graciously afforded to you. And if you'd like to be paired with another man or two, be sure you find this amazing ministry and their website.

Sometimes for extended periods of time, even for hours, I set fixed prayer times without the day, and started to worship during that time and other times too. Almost immediately I could feel this radical change happening deep in my heart once I had been humbled by the exposure of my sin, my Pharisee-like lifestyle and was leaving that life of sin. It was like surgery in my spirit (and I know seems strange to say).

It was also during this time that I found out about marriage restoration, recovery from pornography and adultery from a Christian. I learnt that the Word of God is all-sufficient to correct everything. In other words, the Word of God is complete for every situation, every circumstance and every facet of life. The Word of God then became my hope, my healing, my deliverance, my salvation, my maturity and my promised land.

I have to tell you that it was not easy because I lived with non-Christian roommates and also worked with non-Christians who thought I had "lost it". It was actually the opposite, I had found hope! It was during this time that I started to believe that the hopelessness of my marriage and all my sins was not beyond the Word of God, or the power of God to redeem and to repair. I'm sure most of this you can relate to. More than likely you too are surrounded by many people who think you've lost it. But, Brother, I hope you will learn that losing your life is when you will find it.

Matthew 16:23 "Then Jesus said to His disciples, 'If anyone wishes to come after Me, let him deny himself, and take up his cross, and follow Me. For whoever wishes to save his life shall lose it; but whoever loses his life for My sake shall find it.'"

So I want to encourage you to learn the Word, in your bible and also in the books you've received from this ministry. Daily read it and meditate upon all it's truth, but most importantly become a doer of it. Please allow the Word to search your heart and soul and to reach all aspects of your life. I found that this was my only hope. His Word revived me and kept me going. The Word will do this for you and so much more. Jesus said we live by the Word of God when Satan tempted Jesus; He quoted the Word— how right He was! True Hope, real change, amazing resurrection, awesome awakening, and authentic spiritual nourishment is what you will find in His Word.

Psalm 119: 66- 68 "Do good to your servant according to your word, Lord. Teach me knowledge and good judgment, for I trust your commands. Before I was afflicted I went astray, but now I obey your word. You are good, and what you do is good; teach me your decrees."

Psalm 119: 71- 74 "It was good for me to be afflicted so that I might learn your decrees. The law from your mouth is more precious to me than thousands of pieces of silver and gold. Your hands made me and formed me; give me understanding to learn your commands. May those who fear you rejoice when they see me, for I have put my hope in your word. Psalm 119: 80 "May I wholeheartedly follow your decrees, that I may not be put to shame."

Be sure you take advantage of the free courses that we found will greatly expedite your restoration process when you use the built in Journal.

Remain Encouraged,

~ *Patrick in Australia*

Chapter 14

Traveled My Journey Twice

"God is no Respecter
of Persons"
—Acts 10:34 KJV

First and foremost I want to praise my heavenly Husband for His mercy, grace, favor, goodness, kindness, truth, patience, and love. He is the Love of my life and my Everything! Without Him, I am nothing and can do nothing. He is a miracle working God and works wonders. The way He works and the way He unfolds things is truly amazing. There is nothing that He can't do. He is in control of all things and will work everything out for your good. What He has done for me, He will do for you. Work with Him, not against Him. Allow Him to transform you and take Him at His word. His promises are for us all. He loves us.

I was a fool who tore down my house and every relationship there in. I single handedly tore down my marriage by my contentiousness, bitterness, resentment, anger, jealousy, selfishness, alcoholism, addiction to attention from men, partier, negativity, stubbornness, hard-heartedness, controlling, manipulation, aggressiveness, hardness, toughness, nosy, pushy, rebelliousness, not submissive, rudeness, and self-centeredness. Needless to say, I was a real delight and God had His work cut out in changing me, but He did! PTL!

Since I was so stubborn and hardheaded, the only way He could get my attention was to remove what was 1st in my life and most important to me, my husband. It was 31.5 months before God restored my marriage, I had to go through the journey twice, as it takes me longer than others to get things.

Let me begin with something important, since this is my husband's second marriage. Upon reading the chapter, God Hates Divorce in *"How God Can and Will Restore Your Marriage"* for the first time, I questioned if God wanted to restore my marriage. Why? Well, because my husband was married before, he actually remarried the same woman twice, and my husband wasn't divorced from her the 2nd time when we met and started seeing each other. The papers had been filed but it hadn't go through yet. I wasn't the cause of their divorce, nevertheless, I was dating a married man, he was only separated at the time. After reading chapter, I repented of my actions because I was in the wrong. I started thinking that God may not want to restore my marriage because He might want to restore my husband's previous marriage. I knew from "*A Wise Woman*" that since I hadn't been married, I should have married someone that wasn't married before. So, I sought God for the answer and if He wanted me to pursue marriage restoration or if He was trying to restore my husband's previous marriage. He brought back to my memory a scripture He led me to during the first month or two after my husband left,

Deuteronomy 24: 1-4. I immediately looked it up, it says, "If a man marries a woman who becomes displeasing to him because he finds something indecent about her, and he writes her a certificate of divorce, gives it to her and sends her from his house, and if after she leaves his house she becomes the wife of another man, and her second husband dislikes her and writes her a certificate of divorce, gives it to her and sends her from his house, or if he dies, then her first husband, who divorced her, is not allowed to marry her again after she has been defiled. That would be *detestable* in the eyes of the LORD. Do not bring sin upon the land the LORD your God is giving you as an inheritance." I had my answer, my husband's ex did get remarried for a few months before it ended in divorce. I knew based on God's word, He didn't want to restore their marriage, but ours. PTL for His word and His power!

Due to how we began and our sin, there is still a lot of work to be done in our restoration. My youngest step-daughter resents me and has bitterness towards me as she feels like I didn't allow her father to be a dad to her. She is right. I didn't. Let me tell you, we reap what we sow, I am living proof. Words are so powerful, whether it be positive or negative. Please be careful what you say. This is also why my family resents my husband because of "what he did to me and my son, by abandoning us." But, again, I would slander him to my family and by my own words they developed the wrong opinion of my husband.

How did your restoration actually begin?

Now I'm ready to begin. It was June 16th, (2 and a half years ago on a Saturday and the day before Father's Day), when my husband and I had gone garage selling like normal that everything fell apart. While shopping around, I started asking him who was calling or texting him and what did they say, like I always did. I had to know everything, especially when it came to his girls, he has two daughters from a previous marriage. I would never allow him time alone with them or if I did, I wanted to know what they did, what they talked about, and I couldn't stand the thought of them having fun without me. I was totally insecure. (I didn't have a father growing up, so I didn't understand their relationship.)

Anyways, upon returning from shopping, I could tell my husband had something on his mind, so I asked. I had a sense and I just knew, so I said, "You're leaving me, aren't you?" He said, "Yes, I just can't take the negativity anymore." It wasn't a normal departure, or what I would consider normal. I helped him pack his things even though he told *me* to leave. He stayed around for about 2 hours, crying, and kept telling me he was sorry. He kept hugging and kissing me. So I asked him, so "is this it?" and then he said, he didn't know. I asked him where he was going, but again, he responded he didn't know. I said, "You are going back to your ex and kids, aren't you?" (I would always tell him or say, just go back with *her* and be with your kids because that's what you want anyways, you always want to be around them.) Again he said, "I don't know" then he finally left, and later on that afternoon I had a friend drive me by his ex's house and sure enough, there was his truck. I knew it! I knew he wanted her! I didn't know at the time, but it was my words and the seeds I planted for 5 years that lead him to do this. (However, things aren't always as they seem. I would learn this later and of course, the hard way.) I was devastated.

However, there was a part of me that wanted a divorce, I wanted to be single again. Or least I *thought* that is what I wanted, maybe I was trying to make myself feel better. I had always told my husband that once he married me, it would be forever because I didn't want my kids to go through a divorce or get a divorce like my parents, I wanted to be different. This played deep within my mind, but I didn't want to listen or hear it.

The next morning I woke up, and I kept hearing in my head, this isn't right, this isn't right. So, I got online and started searching for help. I found a program that advertised that they could save marriages if you apply their principles. I ordered the material and 7 days later, it arrived. I immediately read the book and listened to the videos. I put into practice their methods, which consisted of calling my husband once or twice a day, sending gifts, cards, etc.

During the 7 days I was waiting for this to arrive, God began to deal with me. I always said I was a Christian but I didn't have an intimate relationship with God, or even know how to have one. I certainly didn't have any fruits, well not good fruits anyways. EEK! He showed me what a nightmare I was to live with and showed me all about my ways. I remember laying on the couch and having a vision of a black 4x10 piece of wood lifting up off and out of me. I felt like a huge weight had been lifted off of me. I cried for days and was so distraught over the person I had become or was. I didn't know that person, it wasn't me. I didn't like it at all. I wasn't like this before my husband and I got married, what happened to me? Why did I change so drastically? (I turned into a person that I didn't want to turn into, I turned into my stepmother and my mother's ways, ways that I observed, how I grew up.) Thus began my intimate relationship with my Heavenly Father.

I started spending time with Him, reading His word, listening to televangelists like Joyce Meyer and others. I would read Joyce Meyer books and the Word and God started to transform me. I lost a lot of weight as I couldn't eat and stopped drinking alcohol, but just for 2 weeks. I went from one extreme to the other, I became the Chief Pharisee.

My parents were ecstatic that my husband left and thought it was the best thing for me. They told me God had someone better for me and my husband never treated me right, always put his kids first, and did whatever his ex wanted him to do. My parents were so happy I was rid of him and that I could now find someone that would take care of me and treat me right. Deep down, I wasn't willing to let go of my marriage, yet, I knew it wasn't right. I didn't want to go through a divorce or make my son go through a divorce like I had gone through as a child. I wanted to save him from that and to stop the divorce cycle in my family. I wanted it to stop with me, I wanted my stepkids to have an example of how to treat their husbands so they wouldn't go through what I have gone through or what their parents had gone through. I knew they didn't have a good example in their lives just like I didn't have good examples. I wanted more for my son and my stepkids. I wanted to restore my marriage for God's kingdom, honor, and glory, for my son and stepkids, and myself, to be a testimony. I knew I had a lot to learn in order to be this example as I didn't know the WAY, the TRUTH, or the LIFE.

Because I am a school teacher and a coach, I had the summer off. My husband's youngest daughter played volleyball for me at that time and attended the school where I worked. My step kids and I were like sisters, we did a lot together and I would take them to every appointment and game. When my husband left, he didn't have any contact with my son or come to see him. My son was devastated and didn't understand. That first year was awful. The youngest step daughter treated me like the scum of the earth. I was made an object of loathing to her and to my husband. I won't go into details about how horrible this was. I would be told how sorry people were that my husband and I were getting a divorce, his daughter said that he and her mom might get back together, I was told the divorce already was a done deal and had gone through, the ex and my husband would show up to games together, sit by each other, and she would sit close to him, put her arm around him, or touch his leg. It was in front of everyone seeing this and they were watching me, and seeing my reaction. However, by the Grace of God, I handled myself in an appropriate way.

Before God got a hold of me, I wouldn't have reacted as I did, like it didn't bother me and just being light and carefree. To say it was hard to go through this, is putting it lightly. It was one of the worse experiences in my life. I was so glad when the season was over, however, I still had to see his daughter at school. I just stayed to myself that year and didn't talk to many people. I told a few people that I was fighting for my marriage and had about 2-3 supporting me, not family members, but the support only lasted for about a year. It hurt so much for people to think we were divorced and say we were. I thought my husband was going around telling everyone this, and I just wanted people to know the truth about the situation.

So, I fought for my marriage for a year, applying the marriage fitness principles. At the beginning, my husband and I texted once or twice a week. But over time, it decreased. It would be a month or so before he would pick up the phone and talk to me, just for a minute. However, when I would see him at games or if he came over to get something, or if I went to his work to see him, he was distant with me and didn't want anything to do with me. I would talk to a counselor, and tell them everything that was going on, and they would encourage me to continue the process at least for a year. I was crying out to God all along, throwing myself on the floor, not understanding why He wouldn't restore my marriage, why He wouldn't give me the desires of my heart, why He wasn't answering my prayers and being true to His word. I knew He believed in marriage, but I started to think He didn't want to restore mine, that He really did have someone better for me. (Nice for me to behave this way huh? Come to find out when He lead me to RMI, He didn't answer me because I had doubt and unbelief, and what was worse, I put my restoration before Him, while I was still drinking and partying.)

After a year of fighting for my marriage, I quit. I became angry with God. I was mad that He wasn't doing what His word said. I just woke up one morning and said I quit, I can't do this anymore. Right before this, guys were starting to hit on me, wanted to spend time with me, and get to know me, or so that's what I thought. So, I fell into the devil's schemes and temptation. I told myself my husband doesn't want anything to do with me, but these other people do, so forget him, his loss.

Everyone had told me to move on, that I was doing the right thing, that my husband was happy, made his choice, and had moved on with his life, so I needed to move on with mine and stop wasting my life away. They told me he was going out and having fun as they would see him out with his ex and I heard about his family coming down and them going out. So, since he was doing these things, I thought it was okay if I did them. So, I did. (However, my husband has control and knows when to stop. I didn't, I would just go wild.) I would go out and drink so much, that I would get myself into trouble, I wouldn't have any control or know what I was doing. Yes, I committed adultery. I went from one extreme to the other, I had no balance whatsoever.

A week went by without me reaching out or contacting my husband, which was unusual, so he sent me a text stating he hadn't heard from me in a while and that he was just ready to file for divorce. I didn't respond. In my head, I was like fine, go ahead, I am done, one day you will regret your decisions. But, he never filed. I continued on this path of destruction, and my husband would text me from time to time. This pattern continued for about 4 months, from the end of June to October.

At the end of October, I was told that the ex and the girls moved out of state, and my husband was to move at a later date. I was thrilled and thanked God because I had prayed for them to move so I wouldn't have to see them anymore or hear about them going out, etc. I felt like this was an answer to my prayers. (Later, I would regret praying for this. But God is in control and He works all things out for our good.)

After this occurred, my husband started contacting me more, he actually called verses texting. Then in November, my husband came to the house to pick up something. By this time I stopped living and doing what I was doing and started asking and questioning God as to why my husband was starting to contact me and reach out to me again. I didn't understand at all, it made no sense. Anyways, when he came over that day, he wanted to be intimate, but I didn't think or feel it was right having done what I had done and him treating me the way he had the past year or so. I was cold toward him. Throughout the month and into December, our communication picked up.

By mid-December, he wanted to come over one night, so he did. We ended up being intimate. Of course, I felt bad because of what I had done, I hadn't told him. During the month of December and into January, things were great. We started to see each other more, and we even spent New Year's together! It was an amazing time and on New Year's he brought over one of our favorite meals we used to share, it was so sweet and thoughtful. I was happy but still didn't know his motives and still questioned God as to why this was happening. I didn't understand and I wanted to.

So, in late January or February, I contacted the counselor from the program I signed up for. I asked him what I should do, which I now know was wrong! I should have gone to the real Counselor. Because this counselor told me that I needed to have a conversation with my husband and tell him that I had fought for the marriage for a year and then gave up and to find out what his intentions are. So, one night my husband came over and I asked him. I still didn't confess to my adultery. He just said he didn't know. That he didn't know his plans. He didn't know if he was going to stay here or move to where his kids were. Of course this hurt, it was like he always chose his kids over everything, still. I felt used and like I didn't matter to him. I felt like I was just there. I felt like I was not important and last on his list of people to see or spend time with. But we continued to see each other twice a month and chat once a week. He was always busy with work or helping other people. Again, he was always too busy to spend time with me, at least that's what I felt and what it seemed like.

So I started to implement the program again but things didn't progress and my husband seemed to distance himself from me again. (One reason for this was because I was pursuing him like the program said.) I would also pray and cry out to God for understanding and why was this happening again. I would ask Him to tell me the Truth and what His will for my life was. I didn't know if He wanted me with my husband or if He wanted me to move on. I just didn't understand why things weren't getting better. At the end of February, I lost my house and had to move back in with my mother, along with my son.

Time went by and things continued to be the same. We would meet for just an hour or 2, be intimate and go our separate ways. I really felt like a piece of meat. During these encounters or after them, the devil really played mind tricks on me and spoke all kinds of things to me.

I had shoulder surgery in May and again in June, I had a really bad health scare. God had been telling me to stop doing what I was doing for a while, but I didn't listen. Remember, I am hard headed and it takes the 2 x4 method for me to get things. Anyway, I made it to the doctor and I was diagnosed with an ED "Eating Disorder" and hyponatremia (low sodium concentration in the blood). I was told that if I didn't come in when I did, then I could have been in a coma or dead! PTL that He saved me! Since I was diagnosed with an ED, they sent me to a treatment center. Immediately, I knew this wasn't for me. I didn't want to admit that I had an ED or needed their help dealing with it. (Later, I would learn from RMI, that going to these type things isn't of God, so I quit going. I knew it wasn't right and it made me feel horrible about myself when I attended.) While recovering from all this, I began searching again for the truth, mostly online. That's when God led me to RMI, this was the end of June, early July.

I immediately got the eBook, *"How God Can and Will Restore Your Marriage."* Upon reading the first few opening pages, it was there that I got the answers to the questions I had been asking God for so long. I was in awe and just amazed! I was so thankful and I couldn't get enough. I just wanted more and more. I wanted to know all His truth and principles. I finally knew that God wanted and could restore my marriage, despite all the mistakes I had made.

Being a math teacher, I tend to like things in a step format. RMI's resources provided me with that, giving me the steps or the road map to the journey. It equipped me with the information and knowledge of how to handle certain situations, so I would handle them in the way God would want me to handle them, instead of the way I would do it. I praise Him for this truth. As soon as I could, I signed up for the *online courses*. I read and read *"How God Can and Will Restore Your Marriage"* and *"A Wise Woman."* These material renewed my mind and it made me understand God's word and His principles in a new light. A lot of the scriptures that these materials contain are the same ones that God lead me to in that first year. Yet at that time, being a new believer and being alone on the journey, I didn't fully understand. I doubted that His word and principles were for me. I didn't believe He would do things for me. I didn't deserve it. I just thought it was amazing how God had tried to teach me and show me the Truth but I wasn't strong enough and I didn't take Him at His word like RMI taught me to do. RMI taught me what it was like and how to have an intimate relationship with Him, and how to make the Lord my heavenly Husband. God in His mercy and grace gave me another chance, another chance to do things right, His way! I am forever grateful.

He transformed me again and continues to mold me into His Bride with a gentle and quiet spirit which is precious in His sight. He loves me so much He didn't give up on me, though I gave up on Him and was angry at Him. He continues to make me the wife, mother, and woman He has called me to be. I finally submitted to Him and surrendered my life. I let go of everything, casted my cares on Him, and I said, okay God, Your will be done, do with me whatever You wish, I am Yours.That's when He went to work! He had to teach me so many things and change me in so many ways, once again. I was a rebellious child, so moving in with my mother, I had to learn how to honor and respect her. I had to learn how to be submissive to my husband and keep my mouth shut. I had to learn how to build my house upon the Rock and His principles. I had to learn EVERYTHING that the RMI resources provided which is mostly scriptures. So, here I was, I knew I had to go through the journey again. However, this time God was in control, not me, and I would finally get out of the way and not pursue my husband.

Another breakthrough was in July, when I started tithing, half to RMI and half to Joyce Meyer Ministries. Prior to tithing I didn't understand why nothing had changed and things weren't getting better. But when I tithed faithfully for 3 months, at the end of September my husband called me on a Sunday and proceeded to tell me he was moving out of state and going to live with his ex and girls again. Though I didn't know this was God moving my restoration forward. I just Praise God for Him teaching me to keep my mouth shut and to get out of my husband's way. I didn't say anything. Yes I cried because I was hurt, but I let him go! I knew nothing I would say would change his mind anyway; he always chose them before anyone else. I was like the last person to know that he was moving, but I was thankful he told me and he wanted to see me before he left, which was the upcoming Friday. (Later, I learned that his oldest daughter and a few friends told him not to move, so I'd been wrong about their intentions). So, I felt like things were just like they were at the beginning, he was leaving me all over again. But I was wrong.

We met on a Thursday, the day before he moved. He told me it wasn't goodbye and that "we would figure this out." We both cried, hugged and kissed. I knew then that I needed to look to my heavenly Husband and not at the situation or I would sink. I knew I had to keep Him FIRST and trust Him, He knew what He was doing, He is in control. I knew He would work things out for my good. I finally trusted Him. I didn't understand fully at the time why He allowed him to leave, but I just dove into His word and the materials from RMI. I learned that sometimes people had to be lead to the slaughter before they get it, I know I sure did, several times. When this happened, I renewed my mind and learned that I wasn't tithing to my storehouse, so I immediately changed that (I actually did this before my husband moved, so things did get better but not great. We saw each other more and spent more time together. So, that is why it was hard when he left and I didn't understand why.) However, I came across the scripture again that says, "he that conceals his sin, will not prosper." I had read this verse several times before, but this time it hit me. I knew that was it! I knew that my situation wasn't better because I was hiding my sins from my husband. I knew I needed to confess, but I didn't want to. It took a lot but I said, okay God...I am going to take You at Your word and do what Your word says, I am going to go out on a limb and tell my husband.

Since this was delicate, I didn't want to do this via phone, so I waited until I could do it in person. Two weeks later, my husband came into town. He wanted to see me. We met and talked about things that were going on, etc. Then, he wanted to be intimate, so I caved in. In my opinion, this probably wasn't the smartest decision. Anyways, he drove me back to my car and upon departing, I said that I needed to tell him something. I knew I had to do it or it would be a month or so before I got another opportunity. So, I confessed. He was hurt and felt used, like a piece of meat. He didn't get angry or raise his voice. He wasn't really surprised and thought I would have done that after he first left. He had secretly hoped that I would have found someone else and moved on, had a new family. He didn't have much else to say after that, but who could blame him. I left, got into my car and immediately prayed. I couldn't move.

God works in mysterious ways, He is truly amazing! After that, He opened the floodgates and blessings started pouring out in my life. All that weekend, my husband texted or emailed me. Yes, things he would say were hurtful, but I deserved it. But I agreed with everything he said and we began to heal. He didn't know if he could forgive me or if he could move on from this. He said he never once did anything or thought about doing anything like that.

Boy, did I feel like an idiot. I assumed or thought that he had and that he was happy with his ex. I would hear about them going out or I would see them together and it tore me up and down. I thought they were sharing a bed together, but they never did. He'd slept on the couch. I reasoned and was told that because he'd been unfaithful it was okay for me to be too! I was told all that I did was okay because we were separated, and I believed it! Deep down I knew it wasn't right, but I wanted it to be, so I justified it in my head. Please don't fall for this trap.

At one point, he said he didn't know if we could move on from here or if it would be better to get a divorce and then start all over. Thankfully for the teachings of RMI and the Bible, I was able to inform him that if that was his choice, I understood and didn't blame him at all. I told him that if he decided to do that, than to please not include me in the process. I told him I wouldn't contest it, hire a lawyer, or sign. As soon as I said that, he never brought it up or said anymore about it. But things really changed for the better, God began to turn my situation around!

After two weeks of being gone, my husband wanted to move back! Unfortunately, with his company, you have to wait a year before you can get another transfer. But I knew God said nothing is impossible with Him. I knew that if it was His will, HE could get the transfer to go through. My husband told me he was sorry and shouldn't have left me alone for so long. He just got tied up in work and kept his mind off of it. I didn't blame him, I knew why all this had happened. I knew why he had left. God had to change me and get my attention. He is a jealous God and He wanted to be first in my life. I just had to learn the hard way and go through things twice.

There is a part of me that thinks that if I didn't give up after a year, because things got bad between us, then God would have restored my marriage before He did. I think this because things usually get worse right before a breakthrough, however, God has a plan, and He needed me to go through it twice. He wanted me to find RMI and rely, trust, and believe on Him to restore my marriage, not me or anything I had done, certainly not that program I was implementing. It had to be in His timing and by His power. He had to do it, He gets all the glory, honor, and praise! He had to teach me His principles and how to build things on Him. He had to teach me how to have an intimate relationship with Him, to make Him my heavenly Husband, and my everything. I am so thankful that He led me to RMI because when my husband first left, I told God that if He restored my marriage, then I would devote my life to helping others restore their marriages. At that time, I wanted to and thought I had to go back to school and get my degree to do this. I didn't know how this would be possible financially. However, He is so good. He saved me from going back to school to learn all the psychology and their methods, which I know don't work. I am so thankful that He has spared me from that because it tried to do away with Christianity. I know that through RMI, I may be given the opportunity to help other women and stand with them so they don't fall like I did. I know God can use my story and me to work things out for good for others and myself. Yes, I am in the Minister in Training program and awaiting to see if I am given the opportunity to progress further. I know He will allow it if it's His will.

As I said, my husband put in a transfer request and said fortunately he knows people high up in the company that maybe could get it to go through sooner. But I knew only God could make it happen if it was His will. I began to hurt for him because he was miserable where he was, he hated it, and his income was cut in half. I hated to watch him suffer. My husband would come back once or twice a month and he would spend the entire time with me! Before it was just a few hours. Our 7th anniversary was Oct. 2nd, and he sent me flowers to where I worked! I was shocked as he hadn't done that or given me anything in 2 years! God is amazing! He sent me a message that morning, before I got the flowers, saying he was sorry he wasn't there to celebrate. I was just thankful he remembered. Prior to that, probably about a week after he was gone, he sent me his favorite t-shirt of his to sleep with. It was so cute. From the moment I confessed my sin, my husband started pursuing me. He would call several times a day, and our relationship started to grow.

All this time, I didn't think anyone knew about us still being married, except for my family and close friends. I assumed that his daughters, ex, and his family and friends thought that we were divorced. Come to find out, nothing is as it seems. They did know. I don't know who told people we weren't married, but it wasn't my husband whom I'd thought.

I had been praying for so long for God to open up the doors of communication between my step daughters and I. My prayers were answered, when the oldest step daughter started reaching out to me.

She even wanted me to come down during Thanksgiving, it was her idea! She wanted me to look at colleges with her. So, God arranged it where I could go down and was able to spend Thanksgiving weekend with her and my husband! It was amazing, it was like time wasn't lost between us. I know God has called our family to be our first mission field, so I am praying He restores my family. I know He will in His time. I am the one who tore my house down and He will help me build it back. I was unable to spend my birthday, which is in December, or Christmas with my husband, but he was able to come visit the weekend after Christmas. During this month, he found out that he would be transferred but didn't know when; amazingly God allowed it to go through! My husband knew he would be moving back but didn't know when. He would tell me he would live with a friend for a while until he got caught up financially, but he would still mention renting our own house. I was thankful that God put that on his mind. He even allowed my husband to start looking for places online and when he came to visit that week after Christmas, we looked at houses together. It was amazing and I was so thankful. When I would become too pushy or try to do things my way or take over, things would get bad. I knew I needed to step back and let my husband be the "savior" of the family.

Let me tell you how amazing and wonderful my heavenly Husband is. My husband found a house to look at online. Being he was out of town, that left me to go look at it. By the second week in January, my husband told me to try to get the place, so I did. We were told that we had it. So, I got online and filled out the application, etc. A few days later, I was told that another family had gotten the house. I was sad, not at the fact that we didn't get the house, but because we would be living apart and my son and I would still be at my mother's. Yet I knew that God was in control and if He didn't want us to have the house, then He had bigger and better things in store for us. I knew that it was His will, I was okay with it. I knew that I must not be ready to have a restored marriage and build my house on the Rock like I wanted. I knew there were things I still needed to learn, and I would pray for Him to teach me.

We continued to look for houses. By this time, my husband was told that he could move back February 1st. He was thankful and so was I. However, he didn't know where he would live. Sunday, January 25th, the weekend before he was to move back, I got a text from the lady who was renting that one house that I mentioned. She told me that the other family had something come up and couldn't go through with the move, so it was still available! (I had a sense that this would happen.) My husband told me to go ahead and try to get it, but that Wednesday, I was told that I didn't make enough to rent the house. (You have to make 3 times the amount of the rent per month. As a school teacher, yeah, we don't make that kind of money.) So, I told my husband and he said, well, what about if I am on the lease and they have my info! Isn't God amazing? He filled out the forms and Friday, January 30th around 1:30-2:30pm, we were told we were accepted! This was the day before my husband was to come home! God is wonderful and works wonders! He wanted my husband and I both to be on the lease! Our prior home was just in my name. It just amazes me how all this is unfolding. God's beautiful unfolding.

It's been a week and a half since my heavenly Husband has restored my marriage. I pray daily that He helps me build it on the Rock and His principles since I tore it down and cremated it and all the relationships. It is going to take a long time for things between my family and my husband to improve. They don't understand why this happened and are angry with him for abandoning my son and I. Most of their opinion stems from when I slandered my husband to my parents and friends. So because of my words and my actions, they have certain opinions about my husband. They are also more focused on the world's ways of dealing with problems and think divorce is okay. My youngest step daughter, who I have not spoken to, still resents me. She feels like I didn't allow her father to be a dad to her. She has a right to feel this way, because it is true. She wants to have a conversation with me and if she thinks I am lying, she is going to call me out on it. I pray that God speaks through me when this time comes, I pray that she sees Him and sees the changes He has made in me. He is going to have to give me His words to say to her. I pray He turns her heart towards me. I pray that He allows me to be strong spiritually and help me teach my step daughters what is good and right. My step daughters are great and they know God. However, I want them to have a personal relationship with Him. I want to help them not fall into the same traps I did. They are typical teenagers. I pray that I may be a positive influence on them. I want them to have a good example and know how to build a marriage, so they don't fall to the devil's schemes. They haven't had a good example up to this point in their lives on how a marriage is supposed to operate or look. (Neither did I and I want more for them and my son.)

Another change is that God is transforming my husband into the spiritual leader and godly man He has called him to be. I pray that He continues to work on Him. I pray that between Him, and my husband and I, we can teach the kids God's ways. They just don't know and I don't want them to perish for a lack of knowledge. I want my husband to be the head of the household which he has never been, not even in his previous marriage. I am asking God to help me submit and respect him and to be an example to the kids so they know how to build their lives on the Rock, that they don't go through the stuff I went through. Yes, I am asking for a lot but I know God is a restorer of families and relationships are important to Him. It is going to take His hand on this and His miracle working power to change my family and the situation. He can do it!

However, I miss my time with Him since being restored. There is a lot of drama that I knew I would have to deal with and didn't want to deal with before God restored my marriage. I didn't want to deal with my step kids and their resentment towards me or the ex and her shenanigans. I knew it would be a huge trial. (However, my heartaches for her and I am sad for her as I know how she feels and what she is going through since she found out that my husband was moving in with me. I pray for her and for God to bring her to a point of brokenness and to find Him. I know hurting people hurt people. I know she is hurting and has been for a long time. I pray for God to intervene in her life and help her.)

I kept telling God, I didn't know if I wanted restoration anymore, I didn't want to have to deal with it. I knew it would be extremely difficult and I didn't think I was strong enough or am strong enough to deal with things. I know that I can do all things through Christ who strengthens me. I can't do it, but with Him I can. I am relying on my heavenly Husband more than ever. He is my number One. The devil keeps telling me, you don't want this, you don't want this, it won't work out, etc. But, I know my heavenly Husband. I know His word and He hates divorce. I know what He has joined together to let no man separate. I cry out to Him daily to help me and change me — helping me to have and feel the way He wants me to, to have love for my husband and family. Even now the devil keeps bringing up how my step daughter treated me and wants me to have bitterness and unforgiveness towards her, and for the things my husband did. I continue to pray for God to erase my memory and help me to forgive again and again: *Lord, forgive them for they know not what they do*. I know He will be faithful to do this for me.

Either way, what kind of encouragement would you like to leave women with in conclusion?

I am so in love with my heavenly Husband, not because of what He has done for me, but because of Who He is. He is my Rock, He is the One I run to, He is my Counselor, my Friend. HE is the Only One on whom I can depend. He is my salvation. I am so thankful, my words do not do justice, and don't express how grateful I am for all He has done for me. He has taken me, the biggest sinner, and transformed me into His bride. I am nothing without Him, but with Him I am everything. I know who I am in Him and I have security and confidence because of what I have in Him, not in myself. All the bad qualities I had, He removed them and replaced them with His qualities. Yes, I still need refining and I still make mistakes. I am not perfect, but I thank Him that I am not the nightmare of a woman that I was. I came to the point of brokenness and allowed Him to change me. He made me a gentle and quiet spirit, joyful, happy, radiant, secure, confident, humble, caring, kind, gracious, respectful, submissive, faithful, no more rebellion or alcoholism, no more addiction to men and attention. He replaced me with His qualities. Again, He is still perfecting those, I am a work in progress. I don't deserve anything He has done in my life because of all the mistakes I have made, but He is bigger and His grace is bigger than anything I could ever do. His forgiveness and mercy is bigger and new every morning. PTL!

How did God change your situation as you sought Him wholeheartedly?

God changed my situation several times, but it wasn't until I found RMI that I sought Him wholeheartedly. He taught me His principles and showed me the kind of woman I needed to be. He had to change me before He changed the situation. Once I found RMI and started doing each thing His way, He turned my husband's heart back to me.

He had to get me to surrender and let Him take over and be in control. Once I turned my focus on Him and pursued Him, that's when my husband started pursuing me, that's when He turned his heart more to me.

What principles, from God's Word (or through our resources), did the Lord teach you during this trial?

I had to learn every principle the RMI resources and God's Word provided. No, I don't know every or all His principles, but I know if I continue to SG, He will teach me and lead me on the straight and narrow. I had to learn to put Him first, to make Him my heavenly Husband, and have an intimate relationship with Him. I had to learn to let my husband go and stop pursuing him, to keep my mouth shut, be gentle and quiet. I had to learn to not be rebellious, contentious, manipulative and controlling. I had to learn how to submit, honor, and respect my husband, and honor and respect my parents. I had to learn how to tithe to my storehouse and confess my sins. I had to learn what God says about marriage and His principles. I had to learn that psychology methods and counseling was wrong. I had to learn how to build my marriage and relationships on the Rock. I had to learn to agree with my enemy and not argue scriptures with anyone. I had to learn to help others and comfort those instead of being focused on myself. I had to learn to keep my eyes on Him and that He is in control of all things, that He allows trials to come on us for our testing, for our good. I had to learn that a lot of times things get worse right before they get better. I had to learn to take Him at His word, to trust and rely on Him. I had to learn that His principles and promises were for me, that He loves me and wants the best for me, He has a good plan for me. I had to learn to surrender my life to Him. Every principle that the RMI resources contain, I had to learn. I didn't have a good example of how a woman was to be or how a marriage should operate, so I turned into what I was exposed to growing up. That is what turned me into a monster.

What were the most difficult times that God helped you through?

The most difficult times were during the first year after my husband left when I found out he went to live with his ex and kids again. Also, when I was coaching volleyball and my husband and his ex would show up to games together and sit by each other. She would put her arm around him or touch his leg, or least it appeared to be so. I would hear about them going out and going on trips together. People would talk and think that we were divorced, but we weren't. The third difficult time, was when I came to the realization that I was mad and angry at God for not restoring my marriage in a year's time. I didn't understand and I didn't think He was true to His word and promises. Another difficult time was when I had to confess my sin of adultery to my husband.

What was the "turning point" of your restoration?

Things in my restoration started to get better when I began tithing to my storehouse and putting down the bottle, so to speak. However, things didn't fully turn around until I confessed my sin of adultery to my husband.

Tell us HOW it happened? Did your husband just walk in the front door?

No, my husband didn't get to walk through the front door because I lost the house a year before God restored our marriage. My husband got a transfer with his job within 4 months of having decided to move out of state, which isn't supposed to happen. They are supposed to wait a full year before they can transfer back or somewhere else! PTL! God put it in my husband's heart to search for a house, where as before he was planning on moving in with a friend. God provided us with a house the day before my husband moved back in state! It was amazing!

Would you be interested in helping encourage other women?

Yes, most definitely!!!

Did you suspect or could you tell you were close to being restored?

Yes, I could tell restoration was getting close and I started to panic. I didn't think I was ready or could handle it. I didn't think I wanted God to restore my marriage anymore. I cried out to Him.

Would you recommend any of our resource in particular that helped you?

For women interested in restoring their marriages, I would highly recommend the Bible, *How God Can and Will Restore Your Marriage, A Wise Woman, By Word of Their Testimony,* and the online courses.

Would you recommend any of our resource in particular that helped you?

God can and will restore your marriage! Trust and believe on Him. Take Him at His word. What He had done for me, He will do for you. Just work with Him, not against Him. Let Him work in His timing, not your timing. He knows what is best for you. He is in control, He knows what He is doing. When things get rough, hold on, your breakthrough is coming. In everything, look to Him and you will make it. Don't take your eyes off of Him or you will sink. Please make Him your heavenly Husband and the Lord of Your life. Keep Him FIRST in all things and He will give you the desires of your heart. He will bless you above and beyond all your hopes, dreams, and imaginations. He is looking for people to bless. Soak up His word, meditate on it day and night. Pray His word back to Him, it will not return to Him void, it will accomplish what He says He will. His promises are for you. You are special and He loves you. He wants you and wants to be close to you. He wants to help you in every area of your life, big or small. Take His hand and allow Him to lead you. Keep on the straight and narrow path. He will give you the victory, just hold onto Him! Thank you my heavenly Husband. I love you so much, with all my heart, soul and mind. I am forever grateful.

RMI and RMIEW has been truly an amazing blessing to me. I am so thankful the Lord let me to RMI when He did. Through this ministry, I have learned how to make the Lord my Heavenly Husband and how to have an intimate relationship with Him. I have learned the importance of putting Him first in all things and surrendering my life to Him. I have learned that He wants to help me in all areas of my life rather big or small. Through this ministry, I have learned how to become the wife, woman, and mother He has created me to be. I have allowed Him to work in me and make the changes He needs to make. I am far from perfect, but I am so thankful I am not where or who I was. He is changing me daily. I am so thankful for this ministry and all the lessons and encouragement it has provided me. If it wasn't for this ministry, I hate to think where I would be. From this ministry, the desires of my heart have returned and my hope was refreshed. I will alwa ys be grateful for the Lord leading me here and the impact the ministry has had on my life.

This is why I am now a Minister in Training. One of my hearts desires is to help other women. I want to help encourage them along their RJ and help them develop a relationship with my Beloved. I want them to come to know and experience Him like I have. I want to help hold them up and prevent them from falling like I did. I don't want them to make the same mistakes and believe the lies and schemes of the devil as I did.

As part of my minister training I was encouraged to submit praise reports both before and after my restoration. Like these:

"He Is in Control"

This past weekend, I was hurt, devastated, feeling unwanted, and not good enough. Satan was telling me all kinds of untruths about other people, the situation, and myself. My mind was definitely a battlefield. I was under attack. I failed at resisting the devil at his onslaught. *Lord, forgive me for failing.* However, my heavenly Husband spoke to me, first telling me how much He loved me, and how much He wanted me. He then told me that He was in control and if He wanted me to continue to hold the position I was holding, He would have allowed it. He told me that He allows us to go through valleys so He can prepare us for something better. He told me that He has to close the door on some things in my life in order to prepare me and help me move forward to something better, to my hearts desires. He has a good plan for me and He knows what He is doing. He reminded me that the valleys aren't easy to go through, they will happen, but they are to strengthen me, and to refine me. He is so amazing when He speaks to us. When He takes me in His arms and I feel incredible peace surrounding me. The experience is indescribable, truly amazing. When we call out to Him, He is there in a moment, encompassing us with His love, giving us everything we need. I just love Him so much and I thank Him for renewing my mind of how He works and how He loves and cares for me, whether the world wants me or not. He reminded me that the world didn't want Jesus, but it didn't matter what the world said about me or if they liked me. What matters is His opinion of me. He is so good. Thank You my heavenly Husband for renewing my mind, and reminding me of all these things. Thank You for reminding me of Your goodness, love, mercy, grace, favor, forgiveness, patience, and kindness. You are my everything.

"Making Me Radiant"

This past Mother's Day, my earthly husband presented me with a card. In the past, when he would give me cards, he would just sign his name after saying "love you." However, in this card, he took the time to write a paragraph in which he stated how much he loves seeing how much I have grown as a mother and as a woman. He loves my passion for the Lord and seeing my joy for Him. He also stated that he loved the fact that I want to be a positive influence in his daughters' lives, which means a lot to him as his kids have been through a lot. Upon reading this, I immediately starting thanking and praising the Lord because it was only Him who has changed me. It was nothing that I had done, but only Him. He continues to change me and I pray He never stops. :) My earthly husband has also mentioned my "glow" and I know it is only Him making me radiant.

I am far from perfect, I am a sinner, the worst actually. However, if He can get a hold of me and transform me, He will and can do it for anyone!

"Become A Cheerful Giver"

I was really blessed by this chapter. It was something that I really needed to learn and take in. Not only do I long for and want to give, but I want to become a cheerful giver. However, I never understood how I could give (especially financially) when I am struggling financially myself. I would hold onto every penny I could and calculate things so I didn't go over my limits I had set. I was afraid I wouldn't have enough money to cover bills or cost of food. This is a huge hurdle that I need to be able to cross. I find myself yearning to help people monetarily, but then I look at my account and my bills and say, "How can I give to them, when I barely have enough to cover my family's needs or my needs?"

But therein lies the problem, I was looking at what I could "see"and asking myself these questions. I was lacking faith, or at least not applying it. I didn't know how I could "do" for others. Well, I can't DO anything without my Beloved! I wasn't asking my Beloved, the One who is the Source of it all, the One who owns everything. I was leaving Him out of this area of my life, not allowing Him to take over my finances and be in charge. I wasn't allowing Him to lead me and show me how He wants me to give in order to be a blessing to others. I didn't realize that it is during my lack, that He wants to increase what I have. He wants to show up in my life and bless me, if I will bless others.

Before this chapter, I always thought that I must give whenever I see there is a need. But this is wrong on my part, God will guide and lead me to give as He sees fit. If there is a need, He can use others to fill and bless that need, unless He is using that lack to get that person to cry out to Him. He doesn't want me going around giving, He needs to be present in my giving and open the doors. However, I must stay close to Him to be able to discern if it is Him guiding me to give, or if it is the enemy trying to wear me out or steal from me.

My mind was renewed as I had forgotten that with each and every trial, test, temptation, or crisis, God already has a plan in place that includes a blessing at the end. He does not want us to think up our own plan on how to get out. Instead, He simply waits for us to come to Him, not in a state of panic or pleading, but in utter trust just as a child would go to a father who could (and would) fix anything! Instead of being worried or anxious about finances, any trials, or lack in my life, I need to rejoice in Him knowing that He is about to increase what I have!

Now I know that it only does this work financially, but this principle of giving works in all areas of our lives. We must give in the midst of our lack as this is when God is saying, "I am about to increase what you have! Now, put your faith to work for you. Believe what you don't see, walk in that faith. Don't pull back; don't begin to fear that you will run out. I am your Source, but I need your faith, shown by your works (walking it out) for this spiritual law to manifest itself."

Now I have learned that by hoarding all that I have, and not giving away what He wants me to, I am behaving unbecomingly and not acting like God's child or the Lord's bride. By behaving like this, I am not drawing others to want to know Him. This is why I must go to Him, repent of this behavior, and ask Him to change me and help me overcome this hurdle in my life. This is an area that I need to totally surrender to Him in order to experience the abundant life He has planned for me.

I thank Him for teaching me more of His principles and His ways through this chapter.

I confess that I have been struggling with giving monetarily when I didn't "feel" like I had the money to give, or it didn't look like I had enough to give. However, I have now learned that He will lead, guide, and show me how He wants me to give. He doesn't just want me to go around giving to everyone and every need I come into contact with. When I give, He wants to be present and open the doors HE opens, as an opportunity for me to give.

I have struggled that it is during the lack that we are to give as God will use this to increase what we already have. We must run to Him and seek His face, speaking to Him about all our concerns, then allow Him to show us how to handle things the way He wants us to handle them. He will take care of us and supply us of our needs. He will increase and give to us, if we follow Him and trust Him by giving when He says and how He says. I need not fear that things will run out or I won't have enough. I need to run to the Source of it all, who will supply my every need and whose supply never runs out.

I will be SG to show me how to give to others. I will be running to Him and speaking to Him about all my concerns financially. I will lay my financial burden down at His feet and allow Him to carry it. I will surrender that area of my life over to Him. I will trust Him completely that He will supply my every need like He says He will. I will take Him at His word, and trust that His principle and way of doing things work. When I see an area of lack in my life, I will know that is Him saying I am about to increase what You have.

Pray with Me: Lord, forgive me for not surrendering my finances over to You and not trusting that You will supply me of my every need. Forgive me for not giving like I should for fear of running out of money. Forgive me for not going to You and asking for help, and trusting that You would take care of me. Forgive me for behaving unbecomingly and not as Your child by hoarding and holding onto everything that I have, not giving it freely, for fear that I would be left with nothing. Forgive me for counting every cent and tracking it, making sure the bills would be paid. Forgive me for not trusting You, that You would provide since I have professed You are my Husband.

Dear Lord, You are all I want, all i need, and all I live for. You are my Source that will never run dry. Lord, I need You more than ever and I want to have more of You. I want to experience You more, and be a good witness for You. I want to help draw others to You. Lord, change me. Help me to act becomingly and like Your bride. Help me to be a cheerful giver, seeking You, and allowing You to lead me and show me how and what to give. Lord, help me surrender my finances over to You, giving You complete control of them, knowing that you will take care of me and supply my every need. Lord, I need help in this area, I have struggled with it for so long. Help renew my mind that in order to see increase in my life, I must give and the more I give, the more You will bless me. Help me to know that when I have a lack in my life, it is You saying, You are about to increase what I have. Help me to wait on You to provide opportunities and open doors to give how and when You want me to. Help me not to be deceived by the enemy nor be worn out by Him. Help me to stay close to You, holding Your hand, walking by Your side. Lord, You are my everything and I thank You so much for this ministry and all the lessons You are teaching me. Please help me to have more wisdom and understand more deeply the meanings behind what I read.

Please help me recall all the things You have taught me when I need them. Help me to become more like You and change me into the new, beautiful bride You want and created me to be. I want to be closer and have a more intimate relationship with You. Show me the way, Lord. Help me in my volunteer work with this ministry. Help me to learn the new ways quickly and to have a teachable spirit. Help me to watch what I say, so that I don't offend or hurt anyone. Help me increase my scores and assignment grades. Help me to do things in Your perfect time. Help me to understand more how this ministry works. Help me to learn and do a better job for You. Give me the words to say when ministering to other women. I can't do it without You. I can't do anything without You. I love You and I praise you so much. I am so thankful.

"You Just Smile & Shine"

Our God is so good and He never ceases to amaze me. Yesterday, the Lord gave me a surprise and I want to thank Him for His blessings.

Yesterday, my husband and I attended a wedding of what we call his adoptive family, as they took him in as their 3rd son and part of their family when he moved to the state we live in 8-9 years ago. This was going to be the first time for me to see most of them since the Lord restored my marriage. So, it had been 3-4 years since I had seen them last.

When we arrived, no one really spoke to me, so the enemy used that to try and bring me down. The mind is a battlefield and that is where he likes to strike me, especially when it comes to people liking and accepting me. The enemy immediately started to tell me, "Look, they don't like you. See how they snub you and don't want anything to do with you?" I thought back, "Well, I can't blame them for having those feelings towards me or not liking me because I was so mean, contentious, selfish, negative, and more before. I wouldn't like me either, and I didn't like myself. It isn't my problem if they don't like me, I know my God does, He loves and cares for me. He is in charge of my reputation, not me. I was like... shut up." Then, I just looked around at the beautiful scenery, and thanked God for His creation and just began talking to Him. The wedding was on top of a mountain, like mine was, so the Lord and I spoke about things that were on my heart. It was great.

So, satan tried to get me down and what he meant to hurt me with, God turned it for my good.

After the ceremony, people came up to speak to my husband and when they saw me, they were like "Oh my gosh! I didn't recognize you!" They said, they had thought my husband had upgraded. lol I immediately thank my heavenly Husband for this because I know it was all His doing and Him changing me. I wanted to say out loud, "Yes, I have been upgraded by my heavenly Husband!" Another lady said, "y'all make me so happy." I just give God all the glory for this because it is only Him that restored my marriage and changed me. I thank Him for allowing others to see His work through this.

I asked one person, "Do I really look that different?" I was told, "Yes, you just smile and shine!" This made me smile the biggest smile and clap my hands because I know that is only Him making me radiant! In the past, I never ever smiled. Now, He has changed me to where I shine and smile. I boast in Him and what He has done! I praise Him for the work that He has done in me and for the work He continues to do in me. Keep changing me my Love! I thank Him so much. Praise Him! All glory and honor goes to Him! Blessed be His Name!

~ *Katherine in Kentucky who like many women, turned into what she was exposed to growing up— she said "I turned into a monster." After confessing her sin of adultery to her husband, while taking His hand, and allowing herself to travel along her Restoration Journey, she began to follow HIs principles. Katherine not only experienced a RESTORED marriage, but became a precious to God with a gentle and quiet spirit.*

Chapter 15

My Wife Returned
a Proverbs 31 Woman!!

"An excellent wife, who can find?
For her worth is far above jewels.
The heart of her husband trusts in her,
And he will have no lack of gain"
—Proverbs 31: 10-11

Mark, please tell our readers, how your marriage crisis began:

With fear... I was losing my business, which meant our income and this allowed stress that crept into our relationship. My wife also had unresolved childhood issues of rejection and pain (that I could not resolve). In addition we had no goals and we lost our friendship because of constant criticism. We became caustic towards each other and then my wife sought attention in other relationships (girlfriends, mother, facebook...but no adultery). She finally demanded a separation of our assets and our marriage and moved to another province of Canada.

How did God change you & your situation as you sought Him wholeheartedly?

I realized I could not stand in her way and that God was all I had left (no children, along a new mortgage that I would never be able to pay off). But God answered my prayers of ridding me of my double mindedness and fear, and I began to learn to be content with Him and not be ruled by my emotions, circumstances or by others.

I learned to seek Him in *this* day (not tomorrow) and to live each day to the fullest as He guided me and my tasks. I learned to praise Him with (in my tears) with my words, actions.... with my sacrifise of praise.

What principles, from God's Word (or through our resources), did the Lord teach you during this trial?

I learned that His ways and thoughts are not mine. That I could not see into the future, nevertheless I learned I needed to still TRUST in Him because He loved me—with all my faults—and that He would rebuild me from the ash heap of my life.

I learned that I would rise from this trial in my life stronger, even better for His purposes and that in return He would get the glory and I would one day have tears of joy with humbleness.

I learned that He allowed this to happen for greater joy to come. That I was in His crucible being purified by the His fires.

I also learned that this was a SPIRITUAL battle and not of flesh & blood, with ruptured emotions, bitterness, indignities, retribution, lawyers, money, cars, and houses. That we are slaves to the *one* we obey...either satan or HIM. We are all slaves to sin (& satan) and are duped in blindness. Yet it is His Word that was and is the ONLY solution to our pain and provides the ONLY hope for our desperate need of joy. And finally, that we CANNOT do it the world's way IF we want tears of joy!

What were the most difficult times that God helped you through?

Living alone in an empty house, cooking for myself and then going to sleep in a cold bed. Waking up in the middle of the dark night alone crying out to Him to spare me for my sins. I begged Him to take this load off me.

Letting Him know that I so missed my soulmate who was now gone.

Then I slowly started to realize to a very small degree the pain, loneliness that Christ felt...that I had helped nail Him to the cross. That God was ultimately in charge of me.

Did you suspect you were close to restoration? Were there any signs?

No, not in what I saw or believed. My wife had wanted to maintain contact and I rejected this plan (thinking she wanted to use me as a crutch to rebuild her new future without me), so I rejected all of her phone calls, texts, emails etc.

What was the "turning point" of your restoration?

My wife texted me that she wanted to talk to me, that she had found the answer. I refused to acknowledge her texting & phone calls (not wanting to open myself to more pain and rejection), but then I got a call from my best friend who's wife said *my* wife was flying in the next day to come to my house.

Tell us HOW it happened? Did your wife contact you by phone or just show up at your home?

I actually texted her to not come, and that she would be disappointed. She responded that it was I who stated that if she wished to speak to me, to not text, call or email but to knock on my door and that's just what she was doing! So I agreed to meet her at a restaurant the next day.

Would you recommend any of our resource in particular that h

The *Restore Your Marriage* book, *A Wise Man* and each of the Testimonial Books. Each of these resources ARE HIS WORD, which cut through ALL the confusion and gave me HIS HOPE for JOY that would come!!

What kind of encouragement would you like to leave other men with in conclusion to what you've already shared?

Men, please understand that He answered MY life long prayers of double mindedness and fear through this dark valley of separation with my wife and soulmate. No, not in the way I wanted to happen because this was His plan. And it was important because He wanted me in His crucible—to allow Him to burn off all the dark secrets and filth in my life. And even while still drenched in my tears, I could still sow seeds of faith knowing that one day I would reap sheaves of joy and have an answer as to why He allowed this all to happen.

Also that what satan meant to harm me, He turned it into greater joy because His ways and His thoughts are so far above mine, so what I could *not* imagine, what He had already done ... for me, a wretched sinner—was not impossible for Him.

And that He so loves me, my wife, our families, the stranger, the sinner, the lost, the lonely, that He will NOT leave us!

And finally, that through Him completing what He started, my wife returned a Proverbs 31 woman, with a hunger for the Lord, for His word and for His ways!! My wife is *not* the woman I married—she is much more than I could have ever imagined. And humbly, due to Him, I am also a very changed man.

Most amazingly, that even when I gave up, He did not give and will not ever give up on us because He is no respecter of persons, which means He will go to the ends of the earth to rescue you, your wife, your children.

~ Mark in Ontario, Canada

Restoration Happened Quickly and Suddenly

"An excellent wife, who can find?
For her worth is far above jewels.
The heart of her husband trusts in her,
And he will have no lack of gain"
—Proverbs 31: 10-11

"The wise woman builds her house, but with her own hands the foolish one tears hers down." Proverbs 14:1, NIV.

Before coming here, I was foolish and tore my house down. I was pregnant with my third child. My earthly husband was completing his Master's degree part-time while also working full-time as an Enlisted member of the United States Marine Corps. I was completely overwhelmed with life. Nothing, not one thing, was going right professionally, financially, emotionally or spiritually. I was just a mess. I was frustrated with the demands that life had placed on me. And because of my earthly husband's military orders, I was away from my family. I had to work to supplement his income, and I had to remain flexible to meet the ebb and flow of his demanding career and I was angry about it. What I did not realize is that my heavenly Husband allowed this war to rage inside of me in order to teach me how to "die to self," and build my life upon the Rock.

My anger and resentment compounded each day with my earthly husband. I often lashed out at him and blamed him for any and everything that went wrong. I was so foolish. One evening as my earthly husband was preparing to go to class and I completely flipped out. I yelled, screamed and cursed at him. I let him know how angry I was that he was going to class and not helping me, his poor pregnant wife, with the kids. I got so upset that I followed him to the car screaming and yelling for all the neighbors to see. The more upset I got, the more he ignored me, and the angrier I became. I got so upset that I jerked the car door open and threw out his backpack. The backpack contained an expensive laptop that he bought me a while back. I threatened to leave and vowed that he would never see his children again. He just left and went to class.

We had several arguments before this one with me yelling and screaming. We wouldn't talk for a few days after our arguments and then it would be okay, until I was upset about something else that was insignificant and the cycle would start all over. But not this time. After the last time when I threw his laptop and made a scene for the all neighbors to see, my earthly husband remained silent and distant. A few days later, I awoke with a horrible stomach ache, my vision was blurry and I saw spots.

My earthly husband took me to the ER to get checked out. During the drive, he informed me that he no longer wanted to be married. He told me he felt like we weren't going anywhere. I asked if there was someone else, and he said no. I didn't believe him.

Once we arrived at the hospital, I was immediately admitted, given medication, and told that they would have to induce my labor and take my son early. I was devastated. I felt that I was being punished for all of the wrong that I committed against my earthly husband. I just knew that my son wouldn't make it. I kept telling myself that I had become a stranger to my Lord through my thoughts and deeds and there was nothing "Christ-like" about me. I even convinced myself that Job who was an upright man lost his children so why wouldn't I lose my child? My son was born almost 2 months premature. Yet, my son not only survived, but also thrived. However, this wake up call was not enough to change me. I was angry again because I felt that my earthly husband wasn't there for me during the birth of our son. This led to another fight. He then boldly announced that our relationship was over, he wanted a divorce and he was moving out the second I returned to work. I was devastated.

I remember calling out to the Lord, begging and pleading with Him to move to change my earthly husband's mind or something. Well the Lord answered, but not in the way that I wanted Him to answer. He did not change my situation; He began to change me! After crying out to the Lord, I googled something on my computer and came across this ministry. I read the words "This IS your Divine appointment. Your life is about to change—forever!!" I ordered the materials and devoured them. I read the book in two days. I cried due to my deep conviction, but I felt light, and relieved as I had finally learned the truth and I was set free!

As for God, His way is perfect: The Lord taught me that His word is flawless; He shields all who take refuge in Him (Psalm 18:30, NIV). He taught me how to let go and to honestly and truly seek Him, and not look to Him for what He could do for me. I learned how to be quiet and content in my circumstance. I was so engulfed in Him that my restoration happened suddenly and I didn't even realize it!

The most difficult time of my restoration came when my earthly husband wanted to have a conversation about developing a visitation schedule and his desired child support amount. I was devastated. The first time it was brought up, I began begging and pleading with him to stay and not leave. We were in the car picking our daughter up from school. I got so emotional that I had to ask my earthly husband to pull over. I ran into the restroom of a local fast food store and wept! I did not cry, I wept! I wept so hard that I did not recognize my face in the mirror. I SG then returned to the car.

Several weeks later, the subject was brought up again. But this time I told him that I knew that He would be fair and reasonable and whatever he decided, I would agree to it. My earthly husband hung his head, walked away and he never broached the subject again. This was also the turning point in my restoration journey, as I began to see and feel my heavenly Husband's hand over my life. While I was dying on the inside, He kept me calm and agreeable. It was amazing to see His words come to life in my life. It was at this point that I began to embrace the opposition that came upon me. I realized that through these obstacles I could see His strength perfected in my life. It was through the challenging times that I came to appreciate my affliction, as I was able to learn His decrees. The harder things got, the more I prayed, praised, and read His Words.

My restoration happened quickly and suddenly. It was soon after I let go of attending church and I found that my relationship with Him was all that I needed to make me happy. One day my earthly husband was planning to move out and on with his life, and then the very next day he wasn't. It is as if we never had this rough patch in our marriage. My earthly husband doesn't even speak about it and instead is planning our life and our future together as a family. He wants us to start our own business and he is complementary.

As wonderful as this change is, I literally don't have a moment's peace because my earthly husband wants to spend every waking hour of every day TOGETHER! I found myself struggling with keeping up with my lessons and volunteer work with RMI. Then my heavenly Husband revealed to me that He had given me exactly what I wanted. My earthly husband never even moved out. In fact, we are relocating to a new state soon. Because things are happening so quickly, we had to move into a teeny tiny apartment until we hit the road later on this month. I was SO afraid that the next time I had to move, I would be alone with my children. Yet now I am simply SO thankful that he knows the desires of our hearts and whatever is up ahead will be a blessing just for me!

I would recommended *How God Can and Will Restore Your Marriage* and also the *Workers at Home* books as mandatory resources for restoring your marriage.

Finally, I would love to help and encourage other women who are on this Restoration Journey. I would encourage every women to seek first His kingdom and His righteousness by seeking an intimate relationship with our heavenly Husband and completely submerging yourself in Him—everything else just falls into place.

"Missing the Solitude After Restoration"

"It was good for me to be afflicted so that I might learn your decrees." Psalm 119:71 NIV

This scripture has become the resonating theme throughout my Restoration Journey. I never thought in all my life that I would be giving thanks to my heavenly Husband for allowing affliction to come into my life. But, if it were not for my marital affliction, I would have not come to know Him as my Lord, Savior, Heavenly Husband, Protector, Provider, and Friend. I would not have learned to put my complete and total trust in Him and I most certainly would not have known the principle of tithing. Throughout this past year, I have been privileged to witness my heavenly Husband move in ways unimaginable. I am privileged to have had the opportunity to trek this pilgrimage with the remarkable women of this ministry. I have learned so much and experienced such closeness with Him and was surprised the He has decided to Restore my marriage.

Yes, my dear, sweet, beloved sisters, I am restored! I thought that I would be shouting it from the rooftops, but the fact of the matter is, I now realize that I am going to miss the peaceful solitude that I shared with Him. It is such a challenging experience to move from being totally immersed in our heavenly Husband to now being restored and again being a wife. This time I am totally committed to building my house on The Rock, and submitting to my earthly husband's lead. This has been such a tremendous blessing and I am so thankful that I was led to this ministry.

So, I wanted to give praise to my heavenly Husband for all of you. Thank you for allowing me the privilege to witness how He is moving in your life. Thank you for sharing your struggles, praises, and breakthroughs, as well as listening while I shared mine. Thank you for your willingness to submit to His call and be humbly transparent throughout your journey.

I will continue to SG as I have yet to complete my courses, but I will submit to His guidance and follow where this journey leads. I love you all so much, and I will continue praying for you and praising our heavenly Husband for you.

UPDATE:
Restoration Baby!!
Born in June

"I am the vine; you are the branches. If you remain in me and I in you, you will bear much fruit; apart from me you can do nothing. This is to my Father's glory, that you bear much fruit, showing yourselves to be my disciples." John 15:5,8 NIV

When I first started my restoration journey I was barren. Barren is defined as too poor to produce much or any vegetation, which basically means unfruitful. My heavenly Husband revealed to me that

I was unfruitful because I was not truly connected to Him. I was going through the motions of being a Christian but I really did not have a true and authentic relationship with Him until He allowed my marriage to fall apart. It was at that time I was stripped of every idol that I worshipped and placed before Him. No job, no money, nothing. He allowed me time to rest. He removed lover and friend far from me and provided complete solitude in order for me to experience Him and His love without distraction or interruption.

It was during this time that I was able to get to know Him as my Lord, then my Savior, and then fully embrace Him as my heavenly Husband. Once I recognized that apart from Him I could do nothing, I totally surrendered my life to Him. I then followed His decrees. I started tithing, I started leaning not on my own understanding, but I began trusting Him with my whole heart and I made up in my mind that whatever He took me in life, and whatever He allowed to happen to me, would be well with my soul!

Once I allowed Him to take over, He began to give me the desires of my heart and restore the things I lost. Now He has gifted me with yet another wonderful blessing, my earthly husband and I are expecting our fourth child!

Children are a heritage from the Lord, offspring a reward from him. Psalm 127:3, NIV.

I am just in awe and so thankful for all that He has done for me. I don't feel like I deserve to be rewarded because I am still flawed but I am humbled that He chose to bless me in this manner. I am SO excited to embark upon this phase of my journey with Him and I can't wait to hold and kiss my little blessing!

Thank you for allowing me to share this phase of my journey with you. I love you all and I am praying with and for you.

Dear Friend, I remember when our heavenly Husband blessed me to find this ministry. I was broken, sad, and my life was in an utter state of despair. My earthly husband told me that he wanted a divorce and no longer wanted to be married while we were driving to the hospital as I was experiencing complications with my pregnancy. I was shocked, angry, and then just lost. I cried out to my heavenly Husband

and he answered my prayer. He led me to the truth and transformed me through the renewing of my mind. He gave me a new foundation and I grow closer and more intimate with Him. It was then that I began thanking Him for my martial affliction as it taught me His decrees and brought me back into true fellowship and relationship with Him. This is when I truly let go of my earthly husband and became content with living with Him and allowing Him to take care of me and my children. Then all of a sudden I was blessed with a restored marriage and it was as if nothing every happened, just one day out of the blue my earthly husband went from wanting a divorce and to move out and on with his life, to spending every waking second of every day with me planning our lives and future. Now we serve as a true testament of God doing the impossible!

The journey that I hope and pray you have decided to embark upon with our heavenly Husband is a divine appointment that He has created specifically for you. He is calling you to come experience His power, love, protection, and provision. He specifically chose you for such a time as this as He is about to perform the impossible in your life, so that you can tell everyone of His love, kindness, and miraculous works. This journey will be filled with pain, but only because you are dying to an old life and old self and in order for you to experience all that He has in store for you, you have to go through the valley, but take courage because He is there, He won't leave or betray you, but if you let Him, He will reveal Himself in a way that will change you and those connected to you in ways unimaginable. I was sent ahead so that I can tell you that beyond a shadow of a doubt, that He can AND He will :)

~ *Cierra in Kentucky is a newly* **RESTORED** *Minister in Training, who now specializes in "letting go" while still Married. Everything changed for Cierra when she realized that all her troubles were due to her unfaithfulness in not tithing— she was allowing the enemy to steal not only from her but her family as well.*

Chapter 17

The Centre of My Life

"An excellent wife, who can find?
For her worth is far above jewels.
The heart of her husband trusts in her,
And he will have no lack of gain"
—Proverbs 31:10-11

Nellie, how did your crisis begin?

My earthly husband had left the house after months of stress and anger between us. It wasn't his choice. In fact he hadn't wanted to leave the home, however things escalated to the point whereby he was asked by the police to leave with all his things and he had vowed he would never return.

Previous to this day, our marriage had been built on sinking sand. There were so many emotional issues we had to deal with in our marriage of 5 years. I was back and forth at my mothers house each time we had a disagreement which displeased my earthly husband every time.

Although a christian my approach to our marriage was one of self righteousness. I also discussed everything with family and some of my friends. My earthly husband was not a church-goer but knew the Lord once. I would attend church with my daughter and mother and he would very occasionally visit.

We grew further and further apart and my earthly husband was pursued by other women. Initially he was flattered but nothing took place. It wasn't until I left the house the final time after another argument to go and live with my mother that he started seeing the OW. I sought a divorce but God would have it that I never went through with it (due to ill health at the time). That's when God started working in my life and showing me myself in the light of His Word.

By the time I returned home (approximately 3 months later) my earthly husband was already involved with the OW. That's when he left the home. I was devastated.

How did God change you & did He change your situation as you sought Him wholeheartedly?

During my devastation God had already started working in my life by leading me home. I was led to numerous websites which supported me at the time, including a standers ministry site. When the time was right, God then led me to RMIEW and this was a turning point in my life. Through the resources God showed me myself in the light of His Word and changed me from the inside out. I became more gentle and calm, less worried and more intimate with my heavenly Husband. He became my centre, my focus and changed the way I thought and acted. During this time I followed the principles and prayed, fasted for my strength and did not contact my earthly husband.

What principles, from God's Word (or through our resources), did the Lord teach you during this trial?

The Lord taught me respect, he showed me the 'line management' of respect and my role as a wife and mother.

He showed me how to have a calm, quiet spirit and how to run to Him with my troubles and not my earthly husband.

He taught me the importance of having Him as number 1 and spending time with Him to have that peace and joy He speaks about in His Word.

What were the most difficult times that God helped you through?

The most difficult times the Lord helped me through was when my earthly husband left and I found out there was OW. I would hear things even though I didn't know where he was. It seemed he was happy and it took faith for me to let go completely and devote my life to my heavenly Husband during this time.

Another difficult time was when our daughter would ask questions and I didn't have the answers to give her as my earthly husband was away from us for 13+ months. The Lord provided me with the insight to answer and get through these times.

What was the "turning point" of your restoration?

The turning point for me was completely letting go of my earthly husband and centering my focus on the Lord. This wasn't easy but necessary I believe for the restoration of my marriage. Whenever there was contact with my earthly husband, I was courteous, respectful and had a calm and quiet spirit.

Tell us HOW it happened? Did your husband just walk in? Did you suspect you were close?

As I focused more on the Lord and my relationship with Him I noticed that my earthly husband would be in touch with me more. The calls and frequency of his visits increased along with the hate wall coming down. I suspected I was close, but I never wanted to admit it or focus on it. I kept my focus on my heavenly Husband.

Would you recommend any of our resource in particular that helped you (or your friend)?

I would recommend the Daily Encourager, the RYM book and the Encourager eVideos.

Would you be interested in helping encourage other women?

Yes!

Either way, what kind of encouragement would you like to leave women with in conclusion?

Trust the Lord, don't give up trusting Him to work things out. Make Him the centre of your life during this time and leave the circumstances to Him. Nothing is impossible with Him.

I believe my marriage crisis happened for a lot of reasons, but I have always believed one of the main reasons is for me to help others. I believe being a Minister I can minister truth and life to those who are going through what I have been through. I believe with the principles I have learnt, and am still learning that I can help others in pointing them toward their true Husband so He can have His way in their lives and they can be set free, just as He is doing with me.

"Beautiful Butterflies"

This is my first official praise report (the first of many I hope) and I give God the glory for the work He has been doing in my life and continues to do as I get to know Him more intimately.
It's amazing how much He is changing me without me even realising! He continues to teach me and show me His perspective in all things.

A while ago now, I had what I believe is an open vision where I saw a butterfly happily fluttering around my room. It was transparent, but gold and was emitting a gold glow as it moved. I was of course startled, while at the same time scared to blink in case it disappeared. After several flutters it did indeed disappear. I sought my heavenly Husband on this over the next few weeks and now I am convinced what He was showing me.

More recently, I received some news from my earthly husband that would have normally been devastating. In fact, it would have probably opened a door to the enemy for strife and confusion and every kind of evil work! But looking back now, I see the hand of my Heavenly Love in the timing of the news that was delivered to me, and I can only give praise to Him because my own reaction to the news surprised me and confirmed that indeed my heavenly Husband has been working on me. And then I remembered the butterfly which signifies **new** birth after a period of metamorphosis (death of old). Do you know that during metamorphosis there is a stillness, a changing, into something more beautiful?! Butterflies also signify freedom as they flutter freely and unhindered.

I do not doubt that my heavenly Husband is working in me to accomplish His purposes if I let Him. The more time I spend with Him, the more I will look like Him, reflect Him and draw others to Him, including our earthly husband's. (He has a bigger plan)!

I have realised that this RJ is more than I first thought. Ladies, Our heavenly Husband has called us to Himself, we will no longer be the same, but changed and free. For nothing will hinder us for we are changing into His likeness. Let us surrendering all to Him. He is more than able. Our heavenly Husband has a plan for our lives and this RJ is part of it. For me it has been the springboard. I have no doubt in my mind concerning this. So let us rejoice that we are in His will. What better place to be. Knowing in due time we will reap a harvest, if we faint not.

Be encouraged my dear sisters. We are on the **right** path and it is part of His ultimate Plan for us, and for others around us. It will be beautiful. Just like those butterflies!

"Polished Spiritual Lenses"

The Lord is truly my Great Physician and rather than it being something I just say, I can now testify from personal experience that He really is my Great Physician.

Before I begun on the RJ, my life revolved around my earthly husband in many ways. I would plan my life around him, concern myself with him, worry endlessly which brought me much anxiety and pain. What's more, I could feel that this was not the most healthy way to live but it seemed like I had no control over it. It had become the norm because I had been doing it for so long and on top of that, I believed I had to do it, to keep things ticking along. In fact, I didn't know there was any other way.

Not surprisingly, over time the pressure started to manifest physically and naturally. I found it hard to sleep, I was continuously anxious whether at work or at home, I started getting migraines, I had miscarriages, I was very short-tempered not just with others, but also with myself. I could feel my health declining rapidly but had no control over it. And just to mention, nothing was changing with regard to my earthly husband even though in my own mind I was employing a strategy that I thought was helping. In fact, it was the complete opposite.

Things came to a head when I collapsed at work due to what felt like a burst blood vessel in my head, and had to be driven off in an ambulance and admitted overnight for keyhole surgery on my spine to eliminate a tumour, or growth. I knew then that things were not right, but still, after I was discharged (with nothing diagnosed - which was a sign in itself) I stupidly continued in my way and continued to suffer migraines, panic attacks and anxieties.

It wasn't until I came to RMI that God, my Great Physician, started the healing process in my life. He slowly allowed my earthly husband to loathe me and leave, and then open heart surgery began on my heart. He then prescribed spiritual lenses as my sight was completely ruined. These spiritual lenses were strong at first but gave me great perspective and changed the way I viewed myself, my relationships and everything around me (I still wear them now :)

The prescription He gave me was His Word, to consume it daily as a minimum, but as often as required. This prescription had no negative side effects, only positive, one of which was peace, perspective and joy. (I still take this prescription now :)

Regarding my migraines, I don't have them anymore unless I fail to take my prescription regularly. In fact, I use my infrequent migraines as a sign that I require more of my prescription or a polish/change of my spiritual lenses.

I know my Great Physician is not finished with me yet, and I love the fact that I don't need to make a formal appointment to see Him in His capacity of Physician or Counselor. I love that He works on an 'open door' policy with me and I have a personal direct line to Him. He is fast becoming my Husband now and so the stresses, anxieties, and panic attacks are no longer necessary because He is also my Prince of Peace.

I cannot begin to emphasise the importance of going to see this Great Physician, telling Him your story and issues and letting Him take care of you like no other Doctor really ever can. I would not say that Doctor's don't have their place, but I would recommend seeing this ONE FIRST and taking it from there. I can testify that I am healed, continually being healed and free.

"New Perspective"

Before my marriage crisis, I was very controlling and self righteous (despite calling myself a believer). One of the areas I was particularly controlling in concerned my earthly husbands friends and their visiting our marital home. To be honest, I was not in total agreement of their lifestyle or behaviours and as a result they never really visited our home. My earthly husband would visit them instead.

Since my heavenly Husband got my attention, He has given me His perspective on things. I now see my earthly husband friends visiting as an opportunity to show my heavenly Husband's love, and not in a dominating, controlling, preachy way but rather one of wisdom with a calm and quiet spirit.

I look past the issues that are right in front of me, and discuss my concerns with my heavenly Husband rather than portraying them through my negative body language, facial expressions or speech. I also consider this as an attitude of respect to my earthly husband and now he tells me how comfortable he feels in his own home. Opening our home to those who do not know Christ regardless of their situation, is now becoming a joy for me. It is unlikely these men would grace the doors of the 'church' and so this provides an opportunity for my heavenly Husband to minister His love to them through me - what a privilege!

Not only has my relationship with my heavenly Husband changed, but the dynamic of my relationship with my earthly husband and his friends community has been impacted positively. I trust my heavenly Husband entirely with the final result and no longer look at the circumstances and things that might frustrate me, but rather through my new 'faith lenses!' I believe and know that my heavenly Husband has my best interests and their best interests, and if I surrender to Him will work through me to fulfil His plans in my life and theirs. Amen!!

I had such a debilitating migraine today that I could do nothing but lay down. I seemed to have run out of painkillers and the ones I did have weren't working. I looked to Him and prayed. Within the hour the pain subsided enough for me to continue my day.

"I sought the LORD, and he answered me; he delivered me from all my fears." Psalm 34:4 (KJV)

"The Pain of Letting Go"

I want to praise my Heavenly Love for loving me so much that He took the time to get my attention in order to put me back on the path that I had strayed from, unbeknown to me. What seemed like a crisis to my natural eye (my marriage breakdown) was in fact the very means He used to get my full attention, rebuild my thought life and mind to align with His.

This RJ has brought me into an intimate relationship with my Heavenly Love. Without the crisis, I would not have got to know Him intimately. I love Him like never before. He indeed got my attention and led me to RMI when I was ready, where the resources and website served as supporting tools in my RJ. The crisis served to break me, to the point where I could hear my Heavenly Love, His guidance and direction. He showed me myself gently in the light of His Word and turned me inside out, rebuilding my thought life, my focus, and setting me on the path of my destiny by allowing me to use my crisis as a testimony to minister reconciliation to others.

The letting go was hard for my natural man, but was necessary in order for Him to do the work that was needed in me. It was a process that was painful - reflecting the crucifixion of flesh and everything fleshy and resurrecting my spiritual man.

It sounds cliche, but I am no longer the same. My old man is dying slowly and I am becoming that new creature. The principles He has instilled in me, the focus I now have and His revelatory knowledge mean that He is first place in my life - and this being what He wanted all along. For me to Know Him. The living Word.

It can seem daunting when we are going through hardship, but knowing the Truth really does set you free. Knowing that this crisis was what He used to gain intimacy with me is an overwhelming thought that now makes me smile.

I continue to walk with Him, spend time with Him and be led of Him. He has now become a part of my every day. I know Him and He knows me. I have not arrived, but I am closer to Him and on the right path again with Him leading and guiding me now.

The pain of letting go was necessary. A necessary part of the process, and I continue to let go daily; of myself to Him knowing that the letting go process is what brings me into a closer relationship with Him while He takes care of every aspect of my life. Just like the birds and the flowers, much more me. O the freedom, the peace that comes from knowing Him. This is where He wants us, His children, His brides. He is worthy of all the praise and indeed His ways are past finding out.

What I thought was my worst nightmare was in fact the start of a dream come true. The start of my live personal restoration journey with my Heavenly Husbandman.

Trust in the Lord with all thine heart and lean not on your own understanding . (Prov 3:5)

What looks to the natural eye as a crisis in fact is the very thing our Heavenly Husband uses to get our attention and draw us to Him. It is the start of our intimate relationship with Him.

...Yet not my will but yours be done (Luke 22.42 KJV)

...Father I place my life in our hands (Luke 23.46 KJV)

Letting go (of our will) is the start of releasing ourselves into His care for Him to begin the work of restoration and reconciliation, reordering and rebuilding of our lives and those we come into contact with. Letting go in the natural, is the hardest but equally the necessary part because we are letting go to Him which brings freedom, peace and spiritual intimacy.

But seek ye first the kingdom of God, and his righteousness; and all these things shall be added unto you - Matt 6.33 (KJV)

Seek Him first and He will take care of your needs in His time.

"Made in His image"

I am amazed at how my Heavenly Love and I are communicating on this restoration journey. We are becoming more and more intimate and very recently, He permitted me to catch a glimpse of Him and I want to use this Praise Report to tell you lovely ladies all about how He allowed me to see a part of Him that has resulted in me loving Him even more.

I have been studying the lessons regarding how our Heavenly Love created mankind male and female, and how He created them in HIS image. As I meditated on His Word and the deeper meaning of what this meant, my Heavenly Love allowed me to catch a glimpse of Him.

In further studying the male and female roles and qualities from His Word, and how He made them in HIS image, He revealed to me that He too is made up of these qualities (and roles) found in both the male and the female. So, for example, He has a gentle, quiet quality (female), in addition to a leadership, Head role (male). He has the quality of humility and submission (female) as well as the ability to love (male) - to be honest, He is love! And as He continued to reveal the qualities and roles of each sex, He revealed a part of Himself and I caught a glimpse of Him. Oh how marvellous that my Heavenly Love possesses so many qualities and roles of the male and female sex. He is all of this and we are made in HIS image.

It then got me thinking that this is even more reason for us to embrace being female. By exhibiting and living these qualities and roles out i.e. those outlined in the Word, not only do we live as we were created to be, but by living and walking it out, we shine a part of Him in this life, on earth, for others to see. It is critical therefore that we submit to the roles He has given us as females. We should in fact celebrate our female qualities as we reflect Him when we do so. The same goes for the male. And as we live together, male and female, we will reflect Him, or at least a part of Him on earth. Amazing!

Ladies, our Heavenly Love wants so much to have this intimate relationship with us so He can reveal Himself to us, as well as His will for our lives. The Bible tells us to draw close to Him and He will draw close to us. I know there is so much more of Himself that He wants to reveal to me and I am excited to know Him and to see Him, as I fall deeper in love with Him. How intimate and loving for Him to give me a glimpse of Him. He is so romantic.

"So God created mankind in his own image, in the image of God he created them; male and female he created them." (Genesis 1:27 NIV)

"Whoever has my commands and keeps them is the one who loves me. The one who loves me will be loved by my Father and I too will love

them and show (emphanizō, appear, be manifest, make known) myself to them." (John 14:21 NIV)

"Ministering Opportunities"

I wanted to talk today about how my Heavenly Love has been using me to minister to others. The example I want to share concerns how He allowed me to minister to a colleague at work resulting in me offering them a copy of the book *How God can and will Restore your Marriage* and us becoming and encouraging support to each other at work.

We have been going through a relatively unsettling time at work with various redundancies and relocations and I have used the time to draw closer to my heavenly Husband so that I can be a light and encouragement to others as He chooses. This particular day there was a meeting in my calendar with 2 of my colleagues however at the very last minute one of them cancelled. I deliberated whether to reschedule however we went ahead and had the meeting with just the 2 of us.

During the meeting it transpired that this lady was having some marital challenges not dissimilar to mine and was also a believer. I was able to use some of the time to minister to her sharing my testimony of what God has done in my life and marriage and give her a copy of the book which she has begun reading. As a result we are able to meet up at lunchtimes and discuss things about God and encourage each to other through the unsettling time at work. I am sure there is so much more that God wants to do as I submit myself to Him and depend on Him to see me through but I am amazed at how He is using me in ministry, even at work. My relationship with Him is so much stronger since spending time with Him and in His Word through the various lessons in Erin's ministry. I am more attentive to His voice and am always on the alert to hear His instructions concerning my day.

"Migraines Healed by HL"

For over 2 years I have suffered migraine. The worst episode was when I collapsed at work and could neither speak nor move. As a result I was hospitalised and underwent various invasive tests to eliminate possible stroke. In fact only morphine was able to successfully reduce my pain and thus was another warning sign to the medics that this was something more serious. Yet a lumbar puncture and CO scan revealed nothing. Months later I was referred to a neurologist as the headaches continued. The neurologist confirmed no cause also even though I was advised to take stronger medication with the possibility of an MRI scan if things continued.

But God. As part of my visit, the consultant advised I complete a 2 month headache diary. I wasn't comfortable with his recommendation for the stronger meds but I was inclined to complete the headache diary and continue with my regular painkillers as and when necessary. I also continued to trust my Heavenly Love.

Whilst completing my headache diary faithfully I noticed that my episodes were less frequent than initially and observed that stress and over thinking seemed to be a primary cause. So I gave my stresses completely to my Heavenly love. Every last one of them. I spoke to Him about them as advised by the Ministry and let them go. If they troubled me, I spoke to Him about them and left it there believing He would take care of it. Within the 2 months I noticed the episodes were practically non existent. No scan, no medication. Just a relationship with my Heavenly Love.

Trusting Him and casting my problems on Him and having Him central in my life allowed Him to manage everything, in His time. My part - to rely on Him wholeheartedly, listen and obey faithfully every instruction.

"Not a Stumbling Block"

I recently was informed of the news that I had been made redundant [laid off] at work. This news was a shock to my system, and although we had expected some redundancies at work, we never imagined the magnitude of the changes. My role was one of many eliminated from the Business, and as the primary breadwinner of the home, I have to admit that I was devastated.

My hope was in my heavenly Husband as I know from past experiences that He has proven Himself to be an amazing Provider, however my faith was shaken as I lost my focus initially and began looking at all those things that would be impacted; our home, my daughters school, our car, etc etc. All the things that in the natural, we have depended upon. After day 3 of the news I had emersed myself in my own emotions and that of my colleagues as reality started to hit me.

After discussing the matter with my heavenly Husband, I began to feel a little better. I knew my heavenly Husband was trying to speak to me, but my emotions were getting in the way of me hearing His voice clearer. One thing I did feel led to do was to call a friend of mine who I hadn't spoken to for a while. Co-incidentally it was her day off work and she proceeded to tell me about a retreat she had just come back from and how amazing God had shown Himself to be in her life. As we conversed, I could feel my stresses and burdens being lifted, and as I told her about my job situation, we prayed together.

As we prayed together, my heavenly Husband started to reveal His plan regarding my marriage and my role as a mother and wife. He revealed that He wants to do a shift in our family and that I should trust Him with His plans for me and the family. He spoke of my earthly husband also and how he wants to raise Him up and position Him as the head of the home even further.

As my heavenly Husband started to reveal His plans and thoughts to me, the redundancy started to make sense. No longer did I see the redundancy as a stumbling block or barrier, or negative thing, but I actually started to embrace the fact that this could be part of God's plan for me, for my ministry, for my family. It wasn't too long ago that I was seeking the Lord for a less stressful and time consuming job so I could focus on Him and His plan for my life as a mother, wife and ambassador of His. My outlook started to change, and did my perspective and my friend bore witness to exactly what I was seeing and hearing.

I believe at times we pray for things, and God has a way of answering our prayers, in His timing, in His Way. Unless we are connected to Him, we may miss what He is saying to us or worse still interpret the situation and blessing inaccurately. I do not know His full plan and what will come of this situation of redundancy, but after communing with Him I know He is working things out for my good if I will just rest in Him and trust Him, listening obediently to Him, seeking Him and walking in obedience.

It was through a time of hardship and the trial of my marriage crumbling that my heavenly Husband revealed Himself to me, restored my relationship with Him, and also my earthly family relationship (immediate and extended). I have already proved that my heavenly Husband power is perfected in my weakness and I know that He does not change and this situation is yet another opportunity for Him to reveal Himself and get the ultimate glory.

"A Beautiful Portrait in the Making"

Since starting this restoration journey, I have gradually given my heavenly Husband access to all areas of my life. As He continues to work with my submission, He continues to reorder my life and my family.

Whilst I admit it is not always easy in the natural (reordering is not a terribly easy process to undergo), I can testify that it is the best thing that has ever happened in my life.

The relationship now between my earthly husband and myself is set on the solid foundation of my Heavenly Love. This has meant more peace, more trust, and more love. Our daughter is happier and the home has become one of respect and love - in contrast to the home of chaos before.

In addition, this has spilled over to the relationship my earthly husband has with my mother - in contrast to before - it is now one of love and respect. Our God is good.

He has taken what seemed to be rubbish and no hope, and is making a beautiful portrait as I continue to submit to Him and trust Him. There are times when it is hard, but these are the times I press into Him more.

I continue to be excited to see what He is up to. I am a more peaceful, less anxious and stressed person now. I am learning His principles and practicing them as He refines and molds me into that which He wants me to be. I love Him oh so much. Coming to this site was just the beginning. Restoring my earthly marriage was just the tip of the iceberg. Bringing me in intimate relationship with Him is what this whole thing was about all the time.

~ *Nelli in the United Kingdom*

———————Chapter 18———————

My Husband Changed Overnight!

"'For the Lord has called you,
Like a wife forsaken
and grieved in spirit,
Even like a wife of one's youth
when she is rejected,' Says your God."
—Isaiah 54:6

My earthly husband left after only three months of our marriage. I was truly the 'wife forsaken in her youth' like it says in Isaiah 54:6. To say I was devastated doesn't even come close to how I felt. All my dreams and plans crumbled around me so fast. I couldn't see a future anymore. My husband didn't just leave, he even moved overseas. So I felt truly abandoned.

For the the first six months after my husband left, I blamed him entirely, but then the Lord broke me....even literally! He took friend after friend away from me, and the last straw was when I fell in my house and badly broke my arm. I couldn't drive for six weeks, and that's when God finally had my attention! There was no one left to run to except the Lord. At this point, I was finally willing to surrender and see things His way.

Once I surrendered I was suddenly able to see all of my sins and it humbled me. No longer could I blame my earthly husband for my problems or my selfish ways. I could see my contentiousness and lack of submission. I truly repented and cried out to the Lord for forgiveness. I even repented to my husband in tears and that's when he told me he loved me and that we could try again. I was so happy! I thought my horrible trial was over!

However, just a day later he rang in the middle of the night and said he had changed his mind! So in deep pain and rejection, I ran to the Lord's arms and received comfort from Him, which was the beginning of Him teaching me so many things including me taking Him as my Husband. Step by step over the next few years, he moulded and grew me more and more.

Over those few years, the Lord taught me that my earthly husband is my head and that I am to submit to him, even when it is scary...because the Lord is the head over my earthly husband and He is in control of everything my husband does so I can trust the Lord to keep me safe. Once I had to submit during our separation to some very hard things, but the Lord was faithful to work them out and bless me in the process because I trusted Him!

The Lord also taught me to let go of my husband and to focus on Him instead. The Lord taught me not look at my husband's sins but at mine. He taught me to pray and trust that He would heal us and our family and restore our marriage and family. I couldn't fight in the flesh but had to walk in the spirit. Another principle He taught me was to thank and praise Him for EVERYTHING, good and bad, because He works ALL things for our good. He showed me the importance of being a keeper at home so I gave up my university degree at my husband's request. All I can say is that I feel so much freer now and for the first time I know I am in God's will. (God also provided a way for me to be a keeper at home while my husband was away which was a miracle). Lastly, He showed me that nothing is impossible with Him; if I would just pray and trust Him, then He could move mountains.

The lessons the Lord taught me were not at all easy. The most difficult times was when my husband, on several occasions, became double-minded in the 18 months before he came home. It was like riding a roller coaster and it felt like it would never end. Then God used a crisis to bring my husband back home. It really is true that it gets really bad, maybe even the worst than it's ever been, just before your restoration is due. So don't give up.

The turning point in my restoration was when I truly let go of my husband, and even let go of wanting my marriage being restored. It was when Jesus was enough for me and I knew I would be okay alone and content with Him, even if my husband didn't come back, that I saw the start of God turning my husband's heart back to me. This isn't a 'method'; it can't be faked to get a result. You have to truly let go and have truly found the Lord as all you want and need. Reading the lesson "Finding Your Heavenly Husband" can help.

My husband had been telling me he wanted to reconcile for at least 18 months, but like as I mentioned, he was very double-minded. So God used a crisis (that we are still facing) to bring him home. The crisis intensified and so SUDDENLY..my husband was on a plane flying from the other side of the world to come home...after years of separation. It was *not* how I expected Him to do it, but God alone knows what we need and what our husbands need to obey Him. And it was through this that my husband changed overnight and never once again was double-minded. He was fully committed to our marriage and every day tells me how much he loves me!!

Let me also say that everyone in my life had given up on our marriage and I praise God for that because HE GETS ALL THE GLORY! Our situation was so impossible that only God could have restored it. The Lord was even so kind that at the start of 2014, He told me my husband was coming home that year and to PREPARE me for it. Ladies, my husband was being double-minded at the time and had 'ended' our marriage again after months of close communication. It didn't even seem possible he would come back that year for so many reasons...BUT GOD is not a man that He should lie, and my husband DID miraculously come home this year!

For women interested in restoring their marriages, I would highly recommend *How God Can and Will Restore Your Marriage*. It helped me so much. I still read it to this day and will continue to read it. Also the online courses helped immensely. They showed me a lot of things I was doing wrong and were so practical as were the "Be Encouraged" videos. I listened to them almost daily at times and often fell asleep to them. *By Word of Their Testimony* was so encouraging. Also *A Wise Woman* is also invaluable and I read that to this day too. I'm also reading *Workers@Home* now that my husband is back. But most of all it so SO important to know His word.

Just as RMIEW says all the time, don't listen to others if it does not line up with God's word and don't trust your marriage and life to anyone but the Lord, He alone knows you and your husband (and children if you have them), and only He can direct your every step in your Restoration Journey. If you listen for His voice only and do what

He says, you will make it through. But if you listen to others you will be lost.

So seek the Lord with all you've got. He will be a Husband to you and He will heal and bind every wound. If you humble yourself and acknowledge your sins, He will change you into His image bit by bit. This process will never end and when God restores your marriage, it is a new part of the journey and in many ways is harder, so learn everything now. All I can say is the Lord is kind and merciful and faithful. He has all the answers for you. Just remember once you are restored that you haven't 'arrived'. It is a wonderful blessing but it is not the end of the journey at all. We need to keep following our Lord and seek Him daily.

"For the LORD hath called thee as a woman forsaken and grieved in spirit, and a wife of youth, when thou wast refused, saith thy God." Isaiah 54:6 KJV

"Lover and friend hast thou put far from me, and mine acquaintance into darkness." Psalm 88:18 KJV

"Wives, submit yourselves unto your own husbands, as unto the Lord. For the husband is the head of the wife, even as Christ is the head of the church: and he is the saviour of the body. Therefore as the church is subject unto Christ, so let the wives be to their own husbands in everything." Ephesians 5:22-24 KJV

"And we know that all things work together for good to them that love God, to them who are the called according to his purpose." Romans 8:28 KJV

"In everything give thanks: for this is the will of God in Christ Jesus concerning you." 1 Thessalonians 5:18 KJV

"To be discreet, chaste, keepers at home, good, obedient to their own husbands, that the word of God be not blasphemed." Titus 2:5 KJV

"For my thoughts are not your thoughts, neither are your ways my ways, saith the LORD For as the heavens are higher than the earth, so are my ways higher than your ways, and my thoughts than your thoughts." Isaiah 55:8-9 KJV

"Howbeit when he, the Spirit of truth, is come, he will guide you into all truth: for he shall not speak of himself; but whatsoever he shall hear, that shall he speak: and he will shew you things to come." John 16:13 KJV

"But Jesus beheld them, and said unto them, With men this is impossible; but with God all things are possible." Matthew 19:26 KJV

~ Natasha in New Zealand

Chapter 19

Restored Before Christmas

"And all things,
whatsoever ye shall ask in prayer,
believing,
ye shall receive."
—Matthew 21:22 KJV

Good morning women of God around the world. Firstly I must apologise for this Praise Report taking so long, it is long overdue.

Luke 17:11-19 KJV "And it came to pass, as he went to Jerusalem, that he passed through the midst of Samaria and Galilee. And as he entered into a certain village, there met him ten men that were lepers, which stood afar off: And they lifted up their voices, and said, Jesus, Master, have mercy on us. And when he saw them, he said unto them, Go shew yourselves unto the priests. And it came to pass, that, as they went, they were cleansed. And one of them, when he saw that he was healed, turned back, and with a loud voice glorified God, And fell down on his face at his feet, giving him thanks: and he was a Samaritan. And Jesus answering said, Were there not ten cleansed? But where are the nine? There are not found that returned to give glory to God, save this stranger. And he said unto him, Arise, go thy way: thy faith hath made thee whole.

Always give thanks, always."

If come to realise that if we do not give our God thanks we are then saying it was by our own strength.

Philippians 2:13 13 KJV For it is God which worketh in you both to will and to do of his good pleasure.

I became separated from my earthly husband and had been since January. To say my world fell apart is an understatement. Yet I can't believe that I am writing that this is the best thing that has ever happened to me. You see I have found peace from the Prince of Peace who dwells inside me.

When my earthly husband left in January of last year I found out the following month that I was expecting our 5th child. Surely he will have to come back now. Oh how wrong I was.

Proverbs 21 The king's heart is in the hand of the LORD, as the rivers of water: he turneth it whithersoever he will.

I even lied to him saying that I had a job overseas. I use to call him none stop or get the children to call him. This all had no effect. It wore me out mentally and physically since I was pregnant as well.

James 5:16 16KJV Confess your faults one to another, and pray one for another, that ye may be healed. The effectual fervent prayer of a righteous man availeth much.

After reading *How God Can and Will Restore Your Marriage* I could see my faults and stopped placing the blame on my husband. It was then that I found the One who created heaven and earth. The One whom I could call on anytime and Who would not avoid my calls. The One whom would never forsake me or leave me. The One who, in my time of need, was always there.

Deuteronomy 31:6 "Be strong and of a good courage, fear not, nor be afraid of them: for the LORD thy God, he it is that doth go with thee; he will not fail thee, nor forsake thee."

I also read a book which was recommended by Erin called *Supernatural Childbirth* by Jackie Mize. This book is amazing I can't praise it enough (thank you Erin). I had a wonderful pregnancy, no sickness, no high blood pressure, no swollen ankles, and no pelvic pain just a supernatural pregnancy. Thank you Lord.

The delivery was just as amazing! I prayed to God that I would give birth upright and when I arrived at the hospital the bed was tilted up. I also prayed for a quick delivery like the Hebrew women did in the time of Moses. God delivered my beautiful baby boy in 18 minutes!! My son is an angel of calm and gentle in spirit, which was also my prayer.

When I gave birth to my other children I was always very tearful and sad. This, in part, was my earthly husband's fear. But I now have my heavenly Husband and as such, I was filed with so much joy I could burst.

My Lord that dwells inside me He has taken care of my 5 children all under the tender age of 7.

Matthew 21:22 "And all things, whatsoever ye shall ask in prayer, believing, ye shall receive.

You see ladies there is nothing He can't do, we just have to trust in Him and to pray to Him without ceasing.

1 Thessalonians 5:16-18 16 KJV Rejoice evermore.17 Pray without ceasing.18 In everything give thanks: for this is the will of God in Christ Jesus concerning you.

I hear you ask what of my earthly husband. Well he's asleep in our bed as I type. He has been here since the 23rd December when he came to spend Christmas with the children. God who is so mighty beyond our understanding has softened his heart. He has taken care of me and the children. He also calls me to tell me where he is at all times. We are not yet fully restored, the way I hope we will soon be, but now I understand that my journey with the Lord is meant to last a lifetime. And what's most important is that my relationship with the Lord is fully restored!! That ladies should be our ultimate goal, our restoration with God and our relationship with His son, our Husband.

I would also like to thank all at RMIEW. May God strengthen us and our ministry.

Dear God, I love I thank You glory to you name Hallelujah, Hallelujah. Amen

Satan you are under our feet!!!

Psalm 138:2 KJV I will worship toward thy holy temple, and praise thy name for thy loving kindness and for thy truth: for thou hast magnified thy word above all thy name.

~ *Nana in the United Kingdom*

Chapter 20

God Works Behind the Scenes

"But He said,
'The things that are impossible with people
Are possible with God.' "
—Luke 18:27

All praises to God for all that He has done! Words cannot express the joy in my heart. On August 19th my husband put me and our children out of our home for the OW. He told me he didn't want me anymore and he was going to file for divorce. My 4 girls and I moved in with my mom and dad. I spent a lot of time crying and looking for answers as to why. Then God begin to deal with me. I started reading the Word all the time and attended church. I begin fasting and praying. A dear friend of mine and my pastor also fasted and prayed with me.

There were times that things looked so hopeless. There were no calls, texts, or anything from him. Even when I tried contacting him he would treat me badly and told me to leave him alone. Well, I never gave up on God. I knew God hates divorce and I was determined that somehow God would fix it. Reading the testimonies and praying helped me make it through the hardest times.

On September 22, late at night, my husband texted me. I was asleep so I didn't get the message until the next morning! He just texted me out of the blue—I was not expecting him to tell me he wanted to work things out. He told me he didn't want a divorce and he wants to work things out!! He said he was no longer with the OW. And he does not want to lose me. I was so overjoyed.

The girls and I are in the process of moving back home. I would definitely recommend RMI's resources and I want to encourage other women as well. For those that are believing for their marriages—Do not give up! GOD is able to do any and everything! He is able! Do not give up hope no matter how hopeless the situation looks. God works behind the scenes.

~ Shandricka in Kansas RESTORED

Chapter 21

RESTORED on Anniversary

"Enlarge the place of your tent…
For you will spread abroad
to the right and to the left and will possess **nations**
and will resettle the desolate cities."
—Isaiah 54:2-3

I never thought we had a problem in our marriage. Yet I was full of pride, dominance, arguing and directing, but I didn´t see this. Then I found out my earthly husband had a relationship with OW and that he is in love and feeling like he was a long time ago with me. Because of anger, crying, hurting, pressure and monitoring, it ruined our whole world. It was about everything I wanted, everything I had. I pushed him to leave home and didn´t allow him to come back a few times when he really wanted to! I was blind, I thought he had to do something, he had to change and show it to me. I was so wrong, so proud, earthly husband?!

I start to look for answers! Deeply in my heart I knew God can change my husband, my situation, because He is Almighty God, who I was far away from for few years. So I was praying one night with all my heart, really crying in front of Him to change this hopeless situation, to change my husband. I promised Him I'd forgive him if we can start again and with HIM. I wrote some requests on praying web sites, I was seeking God, looking for a solution. Few days after this, I received an email from one great woman with links for this site. I knew it was a sign from God!!! This was the point that has changed my life forever. He has heard my cry and will help me. I read the book *"How God Can and Will Restore Your Marriage"*, that was translated into my language and knew at that moment **I am the first one to be changed** by Him. Not my husband!

I applied immediately principles (at least I tried) one after another. I read the book many times, prayed all days long, I rediscover my relationship with my Lord Jesus and everything was so clear now!! I was so unfaithful to Him since I met my husband. I was very sorry for this and I was feeling now how it feels to be the second one. Now I was in right way for my whole life. It didn´t matter so badly now what and when will be with my restored marriage, I was honestly happy to live again with Him, for Him, my Jesus!! He helped me through, He is so nice, so gentle!!

The Lord teached me to walk with Him, to seek Him and only Him, to talk about everything to Him firstly, to sit with Him, to pray for my needs. Only He can do everything, hear everything, only He knows what is the best for us, for our lives. If you fall down, just get up and reach His loving hand and look again at Him. He understands and He loves like nobody can love. Yes, my Jesus :) The MAN of my life, forever!!!

When things were very difficult, He gave me what I needed for me and my kids, really!! And He send me His Words when I needed it and helped me to forgive and love again, to not blame, to wait on Him. I praise Him!!!

The turning point came when I began apply principles, when I apologized for my acting, my sins, this was the turning point I think. And when my husband felt I forgive him. However he was still confused. I knew, if he is not coming home yet, it has to be His purpose for both of us. I stopped (after reading the book) arguing, blaming or being needy. I went with everything to my First Love. Then my relationship with earthly husband was very friendly and even if it was so hard some days, I had my Jesus!!

Our 5-yr wedding anniversary was coming. I was a little bit sad seeing this date in my calendar, but kept thinking that God will do what is the best for both of us. More than a month ago my husband was planning to be home at that time. I felt peace. It doesn´t matter for me really when my husband comes back. I wanted only he will come when God wants. And He put in his heart desire to be with me again forever on this same day of our anniversary. So he came back and we are family again!

I still pray our God will change his heart to HIM like he has changed his heart slowly to us. I thank Him, I praise Him with my whole heart.

And I want to stay with Him, in Him to be a good wife for my husband, to please the Lord and live a life He has for us.

I would recommend book "How God Can and Will Restore Your Marriage", "Wise Woman", RRR Courses and especially God´s Word, Holy Bible!

Precious women, never lose hope. Our God is God of impossible things, God of everything!! Just seek Him and be with Him, hold Him strongly and don´t be afraid to walk on stormy seas with eyes on Him :).

~Júlia in Slovakia

Chapter 22

I Had to be Broken

"For I am confident of this very thing,
that He who began a good work in you
will perfect it until the day of Christ Jesus"
—Philippians 1:6

The story of us, Phil and Cindy, goes back a long way with a lot of ups and downs. Our marriage was not built on that Rock that we are supposed to build our house and lives upon. Even though when we started dating I prayed a lot about it and my sister and my mother said that God told them he was the one for me I had no clue what the Bible said regarding marriage.

So after a bunch of hurdles and our daughter being almost 2, we were married, this was almost 12 years ago.

Well-let's jump forward. Due to a bunch of living outside of the life that I know God wanted us to live, our marriage fell apart. My husband couldn't tell me he loved me, rarely was intimate (I know we aren't supposed to degrade our spouse, just telling the story) and I sadly cheated a few times on my marriage. I knew I loved him, but didn't know how to feel better about myself. I know now that this is not the way to do it.

After he found out I cheated (my best friend of 16 years told him) I left and hooked up with an old boyfriend. That relationship was doomed from the start. He was an alcoholic, horribly dysfunctional children (one daughter had a 3 year old at 20 and she addicted to heroin) etc.

I learned very quickly that this wasn't how I wanted to live either.

As you can see, I had to be broken. I was a gypsy. Running away from one place to the next for a year. I finally came to stay at my girlfriend's house. I was always alone and when you are alone that much you really start to think. Too much.

It was SuperBowl Sunday and my ex husband was texting me from a party he went to. All the sudden he quit texting. I thought he had met someone or took someone home with him. Whatever the case my brain started working over time.

I looked up his cell phone as we still share the same bill to see if he was texting anyone and ignoring me and I saw he had been texting someone new. They always texted him first, but when he was telling me he was going to bed he was still texting this person.

(My daughter told me later that it was an old guy friend from his younger days, that he reconnected with) but the enemy knew my weaknesses and schemed to use them to further destroy me. However, God was using this to get my attention.

All of this put me in tailspin and I realized that I could lose what was most precious to me. My family.

I looked for prayer help online. I knew I needed to reconnect with God and quick. I needed to rebuild my marriage and my family and do it right.

Praise God I was soon found a site for prayer and someone left me the HopeAtLast.com site.

All of the resources from this site were my saving grace. I learned how to keep my mouth shut (even though I failed at times), I quit texting and calling my husband but instead always let him contact me. And I drenched myself in the word.

In fact I somehow messed up my lessons in order and ended up doing a bunch at once, at times, trying to figure it all out. This was God helping me go over the same lessons again and again, the ones I really needed to renew my mind.

The whole thing, as you can imagine, has been difficult process. My ex went from praying and fasting begging God that I would return to him, to cold and uncaring. I would hear that we weren't meant to be together and are just made to hurt each other, etc.

When my dog died all I had was a text saying "I'm putting your dog down today." This is why this ministry teaches us to focus on the LORD and not on our circumstances. There is a spiritual battle going on and if we put too much on what we see or hear, we are doomed.

Yet, through all of this turmoil I finally learned a lot about prayer. I asked for a lot of prayer and then finally learned what was more powerful is when I prayed a lot on my own. I finally learned that my husband was not the one to blame for our break up, because even though he didn't say it, he was also blaming himself. So I had to pray for him to forgive himself. This is something he has a hard time with. He holds himself accountable a lot. I had to pray for him to have a soft heart for both himself and for me.

On Spring break I couldn't bring my daughter to my house because I found out that my roommate was a huge pot smoker. My ex is a cop and this was unacceptable for my daughter as you can imagine.

So I came and stayed with my daughter at my ex's house. Needless to say, we had a great week. No contention—nothing but fun. I made sure to have dinner ready when he would get home, bought flowers for the table, etc. It was a great time. We even went and had a date night, just the two of us and had a lot of fun.

The turning point was when my roommate lost her job and messed up her unemployment, which meant I had to move. I told my ex and he made a "deal" for me to live with my daughter at his home. This was to allow us both to get our debt paid off. Of course it was not ideal, but my hope was that after the debt was paid off, that God would turn his heart and not want me to go.

So this wasn't the reconciliation that I wanted. I would love to say he said "I love you, come home" but I am "home" yet, instead I am determined to make the best of of this opportunity to remain pure and hope that soon he will ask me stay together as a couple.

Due to living under the same roof, my husband said he seen the changes in me and I am going to continue to take each step and ask the Lord to guide me in each step I take.

The lessons are what helped me the most. It put the books in smaller doses, which help when you have a busy life and so much to learn.

In conclusion, I would say that whenever our husbands are telling us that they don't love us, or don't think we are meant to be together—that's when you need to remember that what God has brought us through, and that it says man cannot separate. Whether we see it or not, we are unified by God as a married couple, therefore we owe that union and be willing to fight for it by doing what is right.

Letting go is hard, especially when you love someone but, if you ask God for that faith, for that mercy and grace, get on your knees and make sure He knows that no matter what comes down in your life, that you will remain steadfast with God—He will not lose you or give up on what He promised.

~ Cindy in Arizona

Ministry Note: We have been in contact with Cindy to warn her about the dangers of living with an ex-husband, knowing the dangers of intimacy before remarrying and the ongoing temptation living under one roof.

We also shared Sabrina in Georgia, which was found in Chapter 1, Newly RESTORED testimony, which we would encourage you to read.

However, each person must walk their Restoration Journey as the Lord leads us, which is why we share the truth and leave the rest to the LORD rather than interfering it in. It's our mistakes that bring about the strongest convictions and deeper understanding of His mercy—which is why we encourage wives not to interfere with the journey their husbands are on.

Ministry Note 2: Thankfully the Lord never fails. Not too long after trusting Him to convict Cindy, it was her husband Phil who felt convicted and remarried his ex-wife. Thank You Lord!

Chapter 23

Seeking the Lord with Zeal

"Who is there to harm you
if you prove zealous
for what is good?"
—1 Peter 3:13-15

Hello, my name is Martha and I am sitting on our bed, typing my restoration testimony :) to share with you!! Here is a little bit about what happened that I hope will encourage each of you!

My husband and I were married 6 months and fought constantly! I was contentious and always right. I mothered him, knew it all and belittled him. Every time I threw one of my tantrums, he was always the one to apologize just to keep the peace and then he "checked out". I lived at home but he wanted nothing to do with me and I was rejected constantly. After a few months and with mostly fleshly attempts, we reconciled and things were better. Then the fighting started again and my attitude was right back to where it was. Then one year after the first time he "checked out", he told me he wanted a divorce.

But Praise God that He changed me and is continuing to mold me more into His image!! My closest friends have mentioned to me how much I've matured. I had an overbearing and nagging attitude and now I listen and don't give my opinion unless he asks! As I sought the Lord with all my heart for His face and not His hand, He turned my husband's heart. He wants to be Lord of our lives!!

The principles that I hold dearest are kindness on the tongue, quiet and gentle Spirit, tithe to your storehouse and seek the Lord with zeal! The Lord taught me that He is my husband and He will never let me down, He will always be around, I can ask Him anything and He will always have the perfect answer. He will never reject me and always love me.

The most difficult times were when we had no contact for weeks, when he would flaunt his new and great life and tell me what I did wrong and why we couldn't be together. It was hard to see our home turned into his home and lose friends.

I believe my "turning point" came after I made my mind up and kept it set to follow ALL the principles in the RYM Book that come directly from God's Word! I had been tithing to another ministry and not my storehouse, I was double-minded by allowing this ministry and another restoration ministry to feed me and I was not writing down verses on 3X5 cards. I started doing those things that I thought didn't apply to me, although RMI taught them! I was deceived!

I then began fasting more, spending more time with God and began re-reading the RYM Book. I decided I would stop dreaming up how our restoration would occur and made my mind up to make God my Husband. I went to Him with my worries and anxieties. I want to say that I would not have been able to do any of the above if it wasn't for God and asking Him to help me.

Just last month after I had a fearful urgency to speak to my husband about our reconciliation, he rejected me! Of course he did though! I went against the principles taught and if you do what you know is wrong, it is a sin to you. Thank the Lord for His mercy. My husband then told me that we would talk about it more in depth the next day or later on in the week, which did not happen.

Slowly he started taking me to furniture stores and asking my opinion on them. I didn't think much of it. In fact I tried not to say anything or give my opinion like I always had. He finally had to say "Please tell me your personal opinion. I want to make sure you like it because if you move back, and that will probably be the case, I want you to like it." I smiled and nodded. I knew that had I been eager at this point, he would've regretted saying that.

Just one week later on his birthday after taking him out to dinner, opening presents and spending additional time with friends, he asked me to come home. He told me he loved me for the first time in 8 months and said he couldn't wait till we had kids! He said he wanted to work on things and that he hopes it works out. So here I am, one day later, sitting on our bed typing my restoration testimony :).

Side note: I also want to mention that I grew up being frugal and always had an opinion about how much was spent on EVERYTHING. I liked setting budgets on everything including dinner and presents. I heard the Lord tell me to really treat my husband for his birthday and I actually had a lot of fun doing it! My husband even told ME to not get him something I had picked out because it was too expensive, it was $45. That was not my husband speaking!

I would recommend the Daily Encourager so we can renew our mind daily, doing the courses and reading and re-reading the RYM Book. We need to be transformed by the renewing of our mind! Also please do not tell anyone about your situation.

In conclusion I want to encourage women to not allow the devil to steal from you any longer. Follow God wholeheartedly, He will be with you. Run toward the goal of making God Lord of your life and never look back. Read the Word so you know what the truth is and what a lie is. Don't entertain the lies! When a lie tries to enter into your mind, replace it with the truth! Guard your heart.

~ Martha in Michigan RESTORED

Chapter 24

He Apologized for Everything!

"Who is there to harm you
if you prove zealous
for what is good?"
—1 Peter 3:13-15

Last January, one week after finding out the MRI results that confirmed our daughter had brain damage from seizures at birth, my husband left me. It all started one night when we were meeting my parents for dinner. We had been through a lot last year, a very traumatic delivery that neither of us dealt with. I allowed my in-laws, who became overbearing, to become the focus of our marriage and my misery. We were sitting in the car one night before going in when he made a comment about one of his female co-workers, who I was leary about. I became upset and was short with him that night.

The next night we had to meet his parents for dinner which did not make me happy. I didn't talk much on the way there, and again was contentious and abrupt. The next morning he asked me why I wasn't talking to him. Although everything in me wanted to talk it through with him, I needed to be right and prove my point and didn't respond. He left angry and I called to apologize. He told me he was over this and didn't want to talk to me at all. He had never been so cold or rude to me as that moment. When I tried to talk to him about it, he was so angry. He said he was done dealing with it and had about all he was going to take.

We had a long hurtful talk where he told me he had been thinking of leaving me for a long time. I was shocked and devastated. He went to stay with his parents for the night. He came back the next day, but only spoke to me about our daughter and slept on the couch. This went on for a week. I blew up in anger and hurt and he said he was going to stay with his parents a few days. This turned into six months; six months of the most hurt and pain I had ever felt, but even more than that it was the closest I have ever been to God.

As God led me on my journey, He showed me so many things about myself I didn't like. He showed me things that I needed to let go of in my past - things about my daughter's delivery and the challenges she still has to face. He showed me how I was allowing others to change me into a person I didn't like. He spoke to me louder than ever and even on my darkest days, and there were many, I knew He told me that He would restore my marriage. I learned how to be still and trust Him.

During my trial, the Lord taught me to be still and know that He is God. He taught me to seek Him first in everything. He taught me how to allow him to heal my hurts. He taught me that nothing is impossible for me as long as I do things through Him. Through this ministry, the Lord showed me how to be the Proverbs 31 woman, which is the kind of woman He intended me to be. I began learning that I do not have to be joyful about my circumstances, but I can be joyful in them.

The most difficult challenge for me was facing divorce, losing my husband and the fear of being a single mom. The courses this ministry allowed me to take gave me such hope during a scary time. God brought this ministry and people into my life just for this trial. Some of the darkest times was having my husband who I thought knew me better than anyone, say such horrible and hurtful things to me. I had to trust who I was in God's eyes to let that go.

The turning point in my restoration is when I had to let go. When I did, my husband began wanting to spend more time with me and our daughter. One night, out of nowhere, he apologized for everything. He began inviting me and our daughter to do more things with him. One day he told me he was thinking of coming home and asked if I was okay with it. (Of course I was okay with it! :)

For women who are interested in restoring their marriages, I would highly recommend the Bible and all the resources that RMI has to offer, particularly *How God Can and Will Restore Your Marriage* book. This book is the primer for all women going through hard times in their marriages and feel that all hope is dead.

I want to help encourage other women who find themselves in darkness. Even in the darkest day, there is hope in front of you. I have been where you are, cried the tears, felt the pain and all along I could hear God whispering to me even when I didn't believe Him. Lean into Him, be still and know that He is going to restore your marriage and He will show you how. I have tears in my eyes and I'm praying just one person will get some hope from my story.

Read how God continued to Restore Stephanie's Marriage below:

"Small Gestures"

I want to give praise to God and just share how thankful I am today. As I listened to my local Christian station this morning, they did a segment call Requestiomony where callers request a song and share their testimony on what the song means to them. I started thinking of how this station and this fellowship inspired, encouraged and held me up during my separation from my EH. I started thinking about how the smallest gestures can change someone's day or even life. A verse, a song, or a ministry like this. My husband moved home at the end of July after a six-month separation. It wasn't a romantic homecoming like I imagined or you see in movies, but it was perfect. Since he has been home, things have been good.

So I continue to seek God everyday in my marriage, for my marriage and even before I speak to my EH. He gave me his wedding ring to put in a safe place but did not put it on when he came home. I must admit, this killed me and in many ways I think the enemy tried to use this to test and defeat me. But from this ministry, I learned to stay silent and pray about it. Last night out of the blue, he asked where I put his ring because he wanted to put it back on! I cannot tell you how this small gesture just made my night! I cried tears of joy and I'm so thankful this morning. I just feel led to share encouragement with others that everything DOES work together for good. There is HOPE in front of you.

Seek God and do not give up. When God places something in your heart, do it, seek Him and believe Him. You never know how the smallest gestures can be reaffirming to someone and can show them that God is real. He does care about each and everyone one of us. He knows your name, He knows what you are going through and you WILL get through this. Be Encouraged! ~ *Stephanie in Tennessee*

Chapter 25

Potter's Wheel

"Who is there to harm you
if you prove zealous
for what is good?"
—1 Peter 3:13-15

In June of this year, my earthly husband walked out on me with no explanation. I was married on June 7th and ten days later my earthly husband left. It left me feeling lost and confused. Although I felt my marriage was over, I had a peace within me which left me more confused. I had no idea that my earthly husband had a drug problem until the night of our honeymoon. I love my earthly husband dearly and wanted him to come home to work on our marriage. However, he would not talk to me. No one believed that my marriage was worth being restored, and many, except one woman, felt I should seek a divorce. None of them suggested that I seek God. While on a prayer room site Ramona, one of the RMI ministers reached out to me and shared the first chapter of "How God Can and Will Restore Your Marriage." I had witnessed two restored marriages, so I knew God was able to restore mine.

I read the entire chapter of the book that same night. It gave me the determination to follow everything God instructed me to do. The further along I walked with God, the more I began to change. God redirected my focus from my marriage to my relationship with Him. I thought that my attendance in church and knowledge of scripture meant I was fine. I didn't realize that I was living a big lie. I gave my life to the Lord when I was young and had a strong walk with Him until I reached college. Since then I returned to the Lord but I struggled with the hurt and lies my church taught me. It was a constant battle between the worldly teachings of the church and my christian walk with God. When He got a hold of me, He removed the dark cloud of sin surrounding my life. I was prideful, arrogant, greedy, bossy, a know-it-all, mean-spirited, and impatient. I was ashamed at how I treated my earthly husband and loved ones. I asked God to change me no matter how much it hurt. I refused to get off the potter's wheel. The Lord beat, shook, pressed and molded me in all sorts of ways. I learned to bring everything only to God and feed myself daily on His Word. I fasted to die to my flesh and eliminated everything that distracted me from hearing God's Word. I allowed Him to renew my mind from years of wrongful thinking.

I sought God in all I did. I allowed Him to use my life as an open book to share with others about the happiness they could have through Christ. There were times when it became hard for me and I became lonely. I tried to fill my loneliness through the company of other men. However, God convicted me to let Him fill my void. Through my trials and testing I learned that obedience to God is the key to a life of peace and joy.

My final test in obedience came when the Lord asked me to take the "How God Can and Will Restore Your Marriage" book to my previous pastor. I didn't understand why. I felt that since she was a pastor, she should know that God can restore marriages. I remained obedient and leaned not on my own understanding. On a Sunday I got up, placed the book in a gift bag, and presented it to my pastor as a gift.

On that Monday, I received an e-mail from my earthly husband at work. We work for the same company and on the same floor. He said he needed to speak with me. Trust me I was nervous. I prepared myself for rejection because that is what I encountered all my life. We met in the middle of the floor. As soon as he saw me a big smile came across his face and he hugged me. He said that he had been praying and wanted to restore our marriage. I stood there shocked and in silence. I told him I had a meeting to attend and he said he would walk me to the meeting. He commented on how quiet and gentle. I was. He kept telling me I was his wife and asked me if I realized it. He said he felt a part of him was missing while he was away from me. My earthly husband thanks God for blessing him with me. He said that seeing and talking to me was the happiest he has been in four months.

Ladies, this was all God. I couldn't have done this alone. I recommend RMI and its resources to all women whether single or married. Please, whatever you do, draw closer to God. Be obedient to all He leads you to do. Follow His Word and the principles laid out for us in this Ministry. It is through our obedience to God that we experience greater blessings, joy and peace that He has stored up for us.

~ *Bonita in Georgia RESTORED*

Now we would like to share with you recent Praise Reports that reveal more of Bonita's speciality:

"My New Heart"

"As the deer pants for streams of water, so my soul pants for You, my God." Psalm 42:1 (NIV)

As I look back over my journey there were times when I did not understand what God was doing and I would become frustrated. As I continued on the journey, He then began to reveal slowly that He was giving me a new heart. Well when He told me He was giving me a new heart, I naturally assumed as I seem to do that He would do it the way I figured, lol! Oh no, God had a way specifically designed for me and it was painful. I have always heard that I needed to die to self and I never understood what that meant until I began to die. The process is very hard because at first my flesh was always in control and if it wanted something I always just gave in because it was in control. I told God whatever it took however painful I wanted to die to self.

As I began to die to myself, I noticed that I was beginning to live, something was changing and I was growing more and more hungry for the things of God and less and less for the things of the world. I hunger to read the Word to just hear Him speak to me even if it is to correct or discipline me, it is wonderful. In the physical, my eyesight is changing and my hearing is changing, so I know something wonderful is happening to me in the spiritual.

God is revealing Himself to me in such a way that all I want is Him and no one else. Yes, I love my earthly husband and thank God for him, but my heavenly Husband is wonderful beyond words!

When I am going through a time of testing or trial, I cry out to Him and He is right there comforting me like no one else can, giving me strength to go through the trial or testing. He speaks in such a way that it makes me bow my head in total worship and reverence because He deserves nothing less. When He shows me my sin, it is so loving and gentle and caring. He never yells or makes me feel like I am a failure, but He lets me know I am showing you this because I love you. See I grew up in a foster home and my sisters and I were yelled at and mistreated daily and as I grew, I naturally assumed this was how God was. And so in my walk with Him, I was always afraid and if I did something wrong I waited for the beating or the rejection.

I am 47 years old, and I am now learning how loving and kind and wonderful my heavenly Husband is to me. Many things had to be broken out of my life because of wrong thinking and past hurts but we have a Heavenly Father who heals and takes away the pain never to be remembered again. I still have much to learn but I now know and understand that my heavenly Husband loves me unconditionally.

"My Answered Prayer"

For awhile my heavenly Husband had me all to Himself, it was just me and Him and it was such a time in which He really changed me and matured me. My daughter who lives with me was helping to take care of my sister who has to have surgery.

Well I had begun to pray and talk to God about me being bored and lonely and even thought about maybe taking a second job. Well as you know He did not want me taking another job seeing as He wants me off this one I am presently on (again in His timing).

Well I talked to God and said I have so much free time I need something to do, so I just continued to pray and left it alone. My niece had to have emergency surgery and she has no one to watch her kids. So my sister and I decided that each one of us would take one of the children, and I took her little boy, his name is Charles.

All I can say is God I so thank you for bringing this little boy into my life and into my home. He is such a joy and I am so enjoying taking care of him. I look forward to playing with him and making meals for him and yes even cleaning up after him, I am in heaven. I have not had this much peace in a long time. Yes, I barely get any sleep and yes when I go to read my Word he is all over me and wants to sit in my lap, but I would not trade this time for nothing in the world. When I am at work my daughter watches him and I find myself asking God if he can be awake when I get home so that I can give him a bath or just play with him. I found myself running through the house the other day and my daughter was like mom I have never seen you run and play like that before. God is so good to me I cannot describe the joy in my heart because He knew exactly what I needed. I have thanked Him for blessing me with this gift. I also know understand what women with children go through when they say they shut themselves in the bathroom just to have some time alone... lol. I know that he will have to go home but while he is with me I am so going to enjoy this time. Our heavenly Husband knows what we need when we need it.

"He is My Source"

My heavenly Husband is so awesome. I know why I had to go through this trial and I so thank Him so much for taking me through this.

I lost my job and my heavenly Husband gave me another one just four days later! Yes, He took my job from me because it had become an idol in my life and He brought me to my knees. I cried out to Him and told Him that I did not want anything or anyone to be first in my life but Him.

When I lost my job fear hit me and it hit me hard, then I started praising Him thanking Him for taking it and something in me just changed I no longer cared about a job, what I was going to wear or what I was going to eat, because I knew without a shadow of a doubt He was going to make a way.

Even if I was going to be like Elijah and He had a raven to feed me I was going to be taken care of. My job is not my source it is just something that my heavenly Husband is using to take care of me His beautiful bride. My heavenly Husband loves me so much He is going to always make sure I want for nothing and as long as I have Him I do not need anything else. I just cannot thank Him enough for taking my job and helping me to grow up and mature more in Him knowing He is all I need.

"Humbled"

I first want to thank my heavenly Husband for allowing me to go through this trial and I am seeing Him work miracles in my life. He has been helping me let go of everything that was an Idol in my life and the biggest was the fear of losing my job, which happened. But oh how He has provided! Not one bill has gone without and I have more food than I can handle, and my family has just been awesome.

As I write this I have tears in my eyes as I think about how much He loves me and how I just did not understand that this trial was designed to bring me closer to Him. I was very prideful in the fact that I did not want to ever have to depend on anyone and that included my heavenly Husband. This was the trial that I feared the most, I would read what other women were going through and say to myself, "I pray God never takes all my finances" but I so thank Him that He has!! I have no money coming in right now but He is handling everything!

He is also teaching me to walk by faith because I used to have to know everything or see it before I would believe it. He is developing patience in me by the things that I must endure and by no means is it easy, but I am determined to go through because I know it is all for my good!

"My Sole Provider"

I am up early this morning and as I am sitting here my heavenly Husband just spoke to me and said "I want to take care of you."

I cannot describe the feeling of love that I feel to know that My heavenly Husband desires me to want for not one thing and I do not :). Yesterday was payday but we did not get paid and I did not even care because I knew He had it all under control. The enemy wanted me to get upset about this and people all around me were angry. I then pulled out my 3x5 cards on my desk and I enjoyed reading His word and renewing my mind. See, I went through a trial and lost my previous job, and during that trial having no money coming, he taught me that He is my sole Provider!!

To know that my heavenly Husband wants to treat me like a queen is amazing because He does not want me to worry or fret or try to figure it out or come up with my own schemes, but just to rest and trust Him to provide for all my needs.

"Being Thankful"

Since going back to work I have not had the time together with my heavenly Husband as I had when I was laid off of work. I have truly missed that time so now I try to get up earlier and spend time with Him because I **need** this time with Him everyday!

Riding to work is a battle within itself, because the place where I live is so crowded and the traffic is scary to say the least. Yet I no longer fear as I did when I first started working because I know that He protects me and shields me from all harm. I now see Him moving in my life to give me time in the traffic to spend with Him, even at work and after work on my drive home.

Let me explain a bit more, where I work the main entrance has been under construction so all of the hundreds of people that work there and also the surrounding businesses are leaving out of just one entrance. During this time of waiting, I now simply pray, listen to music or just sit quietly. At first I confess I was aggravated because it took a half an hour to just get out of the parking lot, but now I see that He is giving me time to spend with Him and I am so grateful!! I am learning so see a blessing in everything. To have a heavenly Husband that loves me so much that He wants to spend every moment with me is amazing. I so thank Him for showing me that many of the delays are just Him giving me more time with Him.

"He Opened My Eyes"

The other day I was doing my lessons and I came across a scripture that I wanted more clarity on, so I started Googling. I felt my heavenly Husband tell me do not do that, but to seek Him for understanding. I had no idea that I was doing anything wrong and was so amazed that even if you Google something you are seeking someone else's answer and not His.

This so changed me into making sure that no matter what we should go to Him for a better understanding. I thank Him that He is showing me how even the smallest act can change my and His relationship. By

Him showing me this has caused me to grow so much closer to Him and also understanding how He wants me to Himself. He also showed me that I was looking for the answer because I still need to be developed in seeking Him for everything, also to be still and wait for Him to answer (I'm still learning to be patient).

I thank Him for these lessons and the check He gives me in my spirit.

"He is My Confidence"

I just want to thank my heavenly Husband for truly restoring back to me my confidence in working. When I lost my job, I lost my confidence in my ability to work or to do a good job. I went through a brief period of feeling as if I was old and how would I be able to compete with the younger generation in the job market. I want to let you know He reminded me that He controls everything and that I am highly favored and blessed and never to look at myself as the world does.

My heavenly Husband has so done amazing things for me on my new job! I have only been at work maybe a little over a month and I want to let you know I am a leader and it is all Him! It is like He took all the training and gave me super powers (lol). Let me explain, I work in an industry where you have to go over people's health benefits with them and you have to be very careful to make sure you are giving the correct information. Well, needless to say, the computer system where I work is so complex. I mean, it is like a maze but my heavenly Husband gave me wisdom that He can only give that it is like I have been working there for years. Everything comes so easy to me, I have the younger people asking for help and now in my work area everyone comes to me for help. Not only do they ask for help at work but they talk about my heavenly Husband and want to know more about Him. It is all Him. I shy away from the attention and tell them He somehow opened my head and put this information inside of me. I am beyond grateful and humbled because I know that it is tough out there in this economy but He has so got me and I pray everyday never again to take my heavenly Husband for granted.

I do not like going through the trials, but I can truly say they are changing me and helping me to be more patient and loving and compassionate towards others.

"Not for My Gain"

As I read my Ministry Commitment's Lesson, my mind flashed back to when I was in church and I can so remember that many times my heart was not right! I wanted everyone to know that I was an awesome Christian and that I knew the word, that is because that was my way of hiding my secret sin.

I always had a struggle with men I believe because I wanted to be loved. Although I grew up with a foster father, he never showed emotion or concern towards me or my sisters.

As I read this I kept saying to myself, *Lord search my heart and if I am serving in this Ministry for the wrong reasons remove me.* I no longer want to serve or do anything for the wrong reason and many times I do have to check myself because it is easy to get over into the flesh.

My deepest desire it to do the will of the Lord, and yes, I struggle to many times keep my focus on Him and not on all that is going on in my journey. After reading this and seeing how many times this Ministry has been attacked, it made me so say Lord help me to be a loyal member and do nothing for my own gain but all for You to help all of us women. I have seen my share of hidden agendas in the church from the pulpit all the way to the usher.

"He Has a Plan"

I just had to write this praise report because my heavenly Husband is doing so much in my life and He is refining me so that I may continue to look to Him for everything I have need of. I have gone through a lot on this journey and I knew that there was going to come a time when He will take everything from me so that I could truly see that He is all I need. I have lost a job and since that happened I am now working but being paid much less than I made before. All this is part of His plan because you see, He has an awesome plan for my life.

Recently I had to move from where I was living because I could no longer afford the rent, but you see, it is again part of His plan. I remember it so vividly, when He began to tell me to move. I kind of sensed it before I even moved into the place, that I would not be there long and my earthly husband confirmed it to me. Trust me, I did not want to hear this because I was so tired of moving and was ready to be still and retire in one spot. But again He has a plan and it is an awesome plan. This plan was to change me into the woman He called me to be before I was formed in my mother's womb. I had to learn to really listen and wait and move when He said so. I had to learn that many times, He does not answer your questions or even reveal what He is doing because see, I had to learn to walk by faith.

Right now, I am totally dependent on my heavenly Husband for everything I have need of and you know what, I am at peace with it. I have never in my life been so happy because He is the one who is in control and He takes care of me so wonderfully. Many would look at my life and say I was homeless and why am I not worried or afraid? Why should I be!! He has always taken care of me and always will.

When it was time to move out of my apartment, I hired movers because He told me to. I did not ask my anyone else. So I hired two movers and He sent four for the price of two. He woke me up early that morning and He told me that when the movers come, He wanted me to pray for each and every one of them. Again, He has a plan. This journey is not just about me; it is about what He wants and when He wants it. He told me the other day that He gave me a truck so that when He says go, I am to pack it up and go. If He had asked me this years ago, I would have fought Him but you see, I do not fight or argue or wonder. I learned to just say yes.

He provides for me and gives me just enough and no more and I no longer have to worry about what I will eat or where I will sleep or even what I will put on, because He provides for it all. Without trying to be in control or trying to fix things, the burden has been lifted off my shoulders, and I am the most grateful person in the world!! My heavenly Husband had to take everything so that I would understand that He is my everything and I am glad that He is doing this in my life!! Oh how it has hurt me. I have been rejected, left, laughed at even felt sorry for but I know not to open my mouth or say one word. I will take it because He has a plan.

"A Breaking Going On"

This morning as I was riding to work a song kept going through my mind, "When Jesus says yes nobody can say no, When Jesus says yes nobody can say no". I then heard the Lord began to say there is a breaking, there is a breaking going on!

I waited and allowed Him to speak and minister to me, as He began to speak He took me to when last week He had me read about Job and He began to let me know that all that I am going through is breaking me so that I can produce more fruit. He says He has and had to turn His face from me and allow me to be broken because He so loves me and knows that I need this. I have lost everything and I sleep on my neices couch and I depend on Him to supply my every need as He sees fit. I have just enough to live on and no more.

Last night, my niece was going through something and instead of talking to others she went in her room and picked up her Bible and began to read. See, she is seeing everything that I am going through, and in my mind I was like "Lord how can this help her when she sees I have been reduce to a loaf of bread!" After she cried and read, she sat down and just opened up to me about things that were so trapped deep inside that she had been dealing with for years, I saw the hurt and the pain and the struggle and I understood and had compassion because through my breaking, He has allowed me to know this pain!! She looked at me and said, "Aunt Bonita, I see all that you have gone through and I see you have such faith." I want you to know that I almost passed out because her seeing me going through and depending on God for everything made me realize that she needs Him more than anything else in her life. I could have prayed, preached, ministered, gave her scripture but it was my life, my walk, my breaking that she saw that caused her to look up.

My life is not about me, I am just a vessel He uses, and yes the breaking is difficult, but I Praise and Thank my Lord that He is breaking me because it is drawing my family to seek after Him. I always thought if they saw the Lord blessing me with this or that or having a big house and cars and money that it would cause them to want Him, but that is not what the Lord wants! He wants us to want Him and need and depend on Him and nothing else.

I am not a great writer, never have been!! I just wanted to share this because I know that it will help someone understand that the breaking is needed and please allow Him to break you and take whatever He needs out of your life so that others can be saved.

"What Is in You"

This morning I was talking to my heavenly Husband and telling Him about how my niece and my husband were saying that I was an encouragement to them, to keep going and not give up. I began to SG because in my fleshly mind I did not understand how I could encourage another when I have nothing myself.

He spoke to me and reminded me that Jesus had no where to live and no where to stay and many times He slept outside but people were drawn to Him and He encouraged others everyday not by what He had but by what was inside of Him.

This was so amazing to me because it delivered me from thinking that material blessing made others think that the Lord was with you. It is not about what you have but it is about what is in you (Holy Spirit).

As I learn to die to self, I am living more and more each day for Him and my life is a light to others for hope and pointing them to Him.

When I was attending church, I was taught that people knew you were a Christian and blessed because they can see the Lord blessing you through "stuff." That is a lie from the enemy because there are those who have nothing but Him and they are so blessed, at peace and full of Him.

"Anything You Want"

Ever since I started my new job, the Lord only allowed me to have just enough. He was teaching me that man does not live by bread alone but from every word that proceeds from His mouth.

I was reduced to a loaf of bread and until He saw fit to elevate me, I had to wait and be content with what I had. I learned to accept whatever He wanted to give me and I learned to not complain but to look at the blessings and the provision as a gift from a loving

Husband. This taught me to be grateful for everything. He humbled me and allowed me to have just enough.

Yesterday at work, I was walking down the hall and He told me, "Today, you may ask Me for anything you want." This was so strong in my spirit; I said if it be Your will can I please have more hours at work (see, I was not getting 40 hours). I prayed and left it at that. This morning when I came in, I was informed that I would be transferring to another team, which will give me more hours and possible overtime. He has also provided a way that I would no longer be staying with my niece but at the end of the week will have my own place to stay. I so thank my heavenly Husband because as I learn to not complain and be content, He is taking me from glory to glory in His way and in His timing.

I am so excited about having a place where it is just me and my heavenly Husband spending that time together so that we can really get closer and closer.

"Any Loophole"

I knew about tithing all my life and it took me going through losing my entire family for me to understand how important it is to tithe!! I no longer tithe to get anything from my heavenly Husband, I tithe because I love Him and obey Him.

I remember when I was in church and I struggled so much with tithing! I would tithe and then I would allow the enemy to whisper in my ear that I needed the money or that it was okay not to because God knew my heart. Yes He knew my heart and it was wicked and disobedient! I wanted to have any loophole to keep from tithing and keeping my money to do whatever I wanted.

I am so thankful and grateful that He did not give up on me and He patiently worked with me and ministered to me that the 10% belongs to Him. I know the struggle of not wanting to let go of the tithe, but I so am grateful that it is not even a struggle any longer.

"I Just Melt"

I so want to sing Praise and Love to my heavenly Husband because He always sends encouragement right when I become afraid or overwhelmed and I am so grateful for His love. This morning as I was reading the Encourager, Sarah in Wales praise report "New Sarah Edwards Chapter: My Journey Home" so encouraged me to understand that what I am going through is all His will. When the heat and the fire are turned up, He is burning all those impurities out of my life.
I just want His will for my life and nothing more. I have lived so long doing what I want but I am more than grateful that He is taking care of me and handling everything. I am at a place in my life where He provides in such a way that it just makes me laugh and smile, and when He speaks to me with so much love and understanding I just melt. To be so loved is beyond what I could ever imagine. I just want to stay with my heavenly Husband because He takes good care of me.

I am just so grateful for the encouragement right when I needed it.

"I Stumble when I Listen to Others"

When I was attending church I always struggled with tithing. There was many times I so felt the Lord dealing with me in this area and I would tithe for awhile and then I would make excuses or allow the enemy to tell me lies. Sadly I'd even heard people in the church who would say the Lord understands that you cannot tithe so give what you can, this caused me to stumble when I listened to others and not the word of the Lord. He commands us to bring the whole tithe into the storehouse for our protection to prove He's first in our lives.

So I was determined that when I came to RMIEW that I was going to be obedient and tithe. Yes, the enemy tried with his lies but I knew the word and I was determined to be obedient. It does not matter if the Lord blesses me with anything, because He said to do it, I am doing just want He said and as a result I have a restored marriage.

If someone would ask me what I would say to others, I would say listen to what the Lord says in His Word and not to others and push past the fear. I have had pastors who would not preach tithing because they did not want to offend people or for people to think they just wanted their money. I had no idea that when you do not preach the whole word of God you are compromising His word, which thankfully doesn't happen here at RMIEW.

If you struggle with tithing, stop and pray with me:

Dear Lord,

I thank you for never giving up on me and continue to deal with my heart about the tithe and how important it is to follow Your word. Lord those times when I listened to the enemy or to others and did not bring my whole tithe I ask you to forgive me.

Dear Fellow traveler,

To bring the whole tithe to the storehouse that the Lord has directed you to. Do not compromise His word but to be obey His word fully.

"Filled a Void"

Today I wanted to just go over the lesson about the Lord becoming my *Heavenly Husband*. I had begun to repeat the phrase "Lord, You are all I want, all I need and all I live for." I know that this is becoming so true in my heart.

I remember that there was a time long ago that I could not wait to get home from work and get on my knees beside my bed and just talk to the Lord. Back then I had no idea that He was my heavenly Husband. I just knew He was all I wanted and needed. Through sin and disobedience I grew apart from the person I needed more than anyone. Yes, I yearned for years to get back to that relationship and when I met people who had that type of relationship with Him I would be so envious. See, I thought I could make a relationship instead of just allowing Him to draw me. I was always caught up in works because I grew up a Baptist and we were taught to work for salvation. This caused me a lot of frustration. My relationship with my heavenly Husband is not something I can make happen. It will come as I read His loving word, take walks with Him and talk to Him. He will become the deepest desire I need.

This morning He showed me it was happening. Over the summer I used to watch my niece's little boy and he was everything to me. I mean he filled a void that only my heavenly Husband should fill. Well I am back to watching him again and this time it is different because there is no void for him to fill because it is filled with my heavenly Husband. This place in me belongs to Him and Him alone. Yes, I love the little boy but I no longer have that void that needs to be filled.

Dear Brides,

Do not try to work at the relationship or try to make it happen, just allow it to grow. Read His loving word, spend time with Him, talk to Him, let Him change and mold you. The relationship will happen if you allow Him to be the one in control. Remember the enemy always wants us to be in works because this causes us to be frustrated and wore out. Remember light and easy.

"Die to My Flesh"

After studying my RMIOU Ministry Commitments lesson, I do believe that I need to read this lesson over and over so that I can truly understand my heavenly Husband.

The enemy has attacked me many times on this journey and I have given into those attacks many times. I have cried out to my heavenly Husband to sense His peace only to come right back and be attacked in my mind again. The battles have gotten so bad that many times I am physically exhausted. I have wanted to give up many times but each time He comes and does something to my heart.

I am now back to living with my niece and I noticed that I have allowed myself to pick back up a bad habit of drinking wine. When I first started this journey I would use wine to cope with the things in my life. I had cried out to the lord and He delivered me, when I lost my job I began to think oh one glass will not hurt, but yes it does, it hurts more than you think because one glass turns into a glass everyday. When I first read this I felt the conviction and I went to my heavenly Husband and prayed. I no longer desire to use wine to dull the pain I now understand that whatever I am feeling good or bad to take it to my heavenly Husband.

I know on this journey many times I struggle with rebellion not because I do not want to do what my heavenly Husband says but many times things He requires are areas I still need to die to in my flesh and it because it's a struggle to let go of those areas because I have allowed them so much control in my life over the years.

I am learning to confess my sin as soon as He shows it to me and not just confessing but asking Him to remove it from my life completely. My desire is to please my heavenly Husband in everything I do and I know many times I have gotten into works trying to make things happen. I am learning to calm down and wait and allow Him to move me forward. It is not easy because I truly want to have my own place to stay again someday. The enemy taunts me all the time about how at the age of 48 I have nothing but it is not about things I know, but it still is something I struggle with.

He says, "If we confess our sins, He is faithful and righteous to forgive us our sins and to cleanse us from all unrighteousness."—1 John 1:9

Lord I confess I have allowed wine to be a comfort to me only to realize that this is not a crutch that I want in my life. I continue to bring the areas in my life that You show me to You so that You can help me overcome. I'm still learning the difference between conviction and condemnation.

Dear Lord,

I still struggle with many times not understanding this journey and many times the enemy tries to tell me I am crazy for following. I have to remind myself of Your word but there are times when he comes at me so hard that I get worn out from the fight.

Dear Brides,

Confess all your sins as He shows them to you let nothing hinder you from making it right with your heavenly Husband so that you can experience His peace and shut the mouth of the enemy.

Ministry note from Erin: I greatly admire Bonita for confessing her "sin" if it is in fact a "sin." I do not drink and never have been a drinker, but I don't believe in itself it IS a sin. In Titus it warns the older woman to not be **"enslaved to much wine."** So if Bonita is feeling "convicted" due to one glass leading to more, and most importantly if this (or anything else we do) is causing others to stumble or weakening her relationship with the Lord, then it is something she should SIMPLY SG and ask Him to remove from her life.

*Titus 2:3-15—"Older women likewise are to be reverent in their behavior, not malicious gossips **nor enslaved to much wine**, teaching what is good, so that they may encourage the young women to love their husbands, to love their children, to be sensible, pure, workers at home, kind, being subject to their own husbands, so that the word of God will not be dishonored."*

"Best of Both Worlds"

I was reading today's Part 3 of the lesson, "Are you ready for a restored marriage?" My marriage has been restored but my earthly husband is not living in the same home due to our financial crisis. I use to worry and pray about this but let me tell you, not anymore. I am so enjoying my time alone with my heavenly Husband. I love it! Yes, I do see my earthly husband all the time and when we see one another, we never argue or fuss; instead we enjoy one another's company so I get the best of both worlds.

I have read the many testimonies of when the earthly husband comes home, all the trials and how many of the women long for that time before the earthly husband comes home. At that time, I could not understand. I so understand now because I no longer long for that. I am so content with what my heavenly Husband is doing right now. I feel so loved because I do not have to face a lot of things that go on with my earthly husband daily as the enemy is constantly on his heels at present, which I know is part of God changing him as He's lovingly changed me.

I have had my eyes opened and I am so grateful for my heavenly Husband for not allowing him to come home yet until He says it is time because trust me, I was by no means ready. I would say please get close to your heavenly Husband and trust me, that feeling of wanting them to come home will go away. We need our heavenly Husband more than our earthly husband. I use to get so upset because of the separation but my heavenly Husband knows what I need more than I would ever know. I love Him for not answering that prayer because He knew what was best for me.

"Where I Need to Be"

I just have to share this because my heavenly Husband knew I wanted so much more of Him and he also knows when is preparing us for something to come.

Where I work is a call center and I do Health and Welfare benefits for a large company. Normally when you work in this type of job you get calls constantly I mean sometimes back to back. Well my heavenly Husband arranged it for me to be on a team that I may get 25 calls a day. So what do I do with the rest of my time, yes I am in my word, praying and listening to him. I pull out my bible and paper and I go to town reading and writing what He places on my heart. See this is my training ground for something to come. I have so gotten to know my heavenly Husband through His word that I see the changes in myself, lol. I do less talking and more listening, which is huge for me because in my family I am one of the talkers.

Can you say being paid to read your word, lol how amazing is that. In my other jobs, to pull out your bible was a big no no but see my heavenly Husband knew where I needed to be and when He sent me to work there I did not want to work there. I was of trying to find where I wanted to work, I so thank Him. He closed all those doors.

I have the best job in the world because I am with my heavenly Husband all day long.

As an antelope pants for streams of water, so my soul pants for you, God. (Psalms 42:1 ISV)

Jesus answered, "It is written: 'Man shall not live on bread alone, but on every word that comes from the mouth of God." (Matthew 4:4 NIV)

When you get to that place in your life that if you do not have Him you have nothing than you are growing closer and closer to Him. I am at that place that without him I have nothing because I need him everyday. I still have a long way to go but I am headed in the right direction towards my heavenly Husband.

"Unexpected Blessing"

My heavenly Husband is so good to me that words cannot describe. Let me begin with the awesome blessing He gave me on Saturday.

I was driving home from work on Friday and my heart just went to my great nephew (he is the one I used to watch). Well he came so strong on me that I just prayed but I knew nothing was wrong because as I was praying I saw him smiling and laughing. So that night I could not sleep and my heavenly Husband just was talking to me about how Jesus had already paid it all He made it so real to me that I just began to weep and thank him for what He had done on the cross for all of us. I went back to sleep for a little while and then again saw my great nephew's face, prayed some more.

I got up started getting ready for the day, making my mental note that I had some grocery shopping to do (now mind you my budget for groceries is 10.00 a week) well this week I had 12.00. I got in the car and started talking about about my nephew and my daughter was like mom I think you are missing him, so I called his mom and asked to speak to him. She was like aunt Bonita God woke me up out my sleep with you on my mind. Well we talked a little bit more and she was like what are you doing today I said well dropping something off at your moms and then grocery shopping. She said, well I am coming to get you and bless you.

Now, this is where the Lord had to deal with my pride because my niece is a single mother with two kids and I do not like her to give or do anything for me because I know she is struggling. Long story short, she had received an unexpected blessing and she had asked the Lord to send someone that she could bless and He showed her me. My niece bought me groceries, took me out to eat me and my daughter and also we all went to a place called Discovery Place where the kids and we all could play, I was so truly blessed Saturday it was unreal. My heavenly Husband did more than I could ever ask or pray for. *"Now to him who is able to do immeasurably more than all we ask or imagine, according to his power that is at work within us"* *(Ephesians 3:20 NIV)*

My heavenly Husband did more than I could even pray or think to pray about.

"Instead, God chose things the world considers foolish in order to shame those who think they are wise. And he chose things that are powerless to shame those who are powerful." (1 Corinthians 1:27 NIV)

He uses whomever he wants, be open because you never know where the blessing is going to come from and when we assume or lean to our own understanding we can miss what He is doing.

"I Began to Fall!"

I took my eyes off my heavenly Husband and when i took my eyes off Him and began to look at my situation I began to fall.

This last week I had begun to get so discouraged and lost my joy and I could not sleep and I just began to worry. I had no idea what in the world was wrong with me, In my mind I was just so ready to give up. My daughter even commented and asked me what was wrong because she could tell that something was wearing me down. I began to pray because whatever this was, was also causing me not to be able to concentrate or focus.

Than this morning as I was getting ready for work my heavenly Husband told me what it was, so simple so gentle, so loving. You have taken your eyes off me and are looking at all that is going on in your life right now and you are also rehearsing every negative comment, and lies, and heartache that you have gone through on this journey.

See right now he told me to be so real because this is going to help someone else, me and my daughter right now are living in and extended stay, I have ten dollars a week that I have budget for food, we survive on frozen meals that do not cost over a dollar. Ever penny is accounted for and yes I tithe. Many would look at my situation and think wow how can you live like that and I will tell you because it is all Him and He does supply all my needs. We want for nothing, food never runs out, gas in my car to get back and forth to work. We find free things to do and we love to window shop (lol)

Well this weekend, I took my eyes off my heavenly Husband, see my earthly husband is working on getting us a house right now and in order to pay the deposit he has offered to work on the house in exchange for reduced rent and not having to put down the deposit. Well I began to look at not having enough money, and how much longer we got to live here and so on and so on as we do when we have allowed the flesh to get in and we have taken eyes off heavenly Husband. I began to sink and I began to sink fast. I cried out to my heavenly Husband and even began to think about leaving the Ministry (trick of the enemy) so many things was going through my mind and all of them negative that it just wore me out, I could not even concentrate to read my bible, so you know it has gotten really bad.

I am so thankful that my heavenly Husband spoke to me and told me what was really going on and what happened. It is so easy to shift that eye and the next things you know both your eyes are on your situation. I thank Him and praise. Please if you have gotten your eyes off your heavenly Husband, stop right now repent go to Him and asked Him to help you get back your focus. He allows us to go through things to help others and ourselves, so now I know when this happens I needed to get my eyes back on my heavenly Husband. Love you ladies.

"Lord, if it's you," Peter replied, "tell me to come to you on the water." "Come," he said. Then Peter got down out of the boat, walked on the water and came toward Jesus. But when he saw the wind, he was afraid and, beginning to sink, cried out, "Lord, save me!" (Matthew 14:28-30 NIV)

As long as I kept my eyes on my heavenly Husband I did not see the raging storm around me but as soon as I shifted my eyes and began to look at all that was going on it so affect my life and I began to sink and sink fast.

~ Bonita in Georgia RESTORED, is a Minister in Training who we can clearly see from her pictures that not willing to get off the potter's wheel can transform you not only on the inside but also what others see on the outside.

Chapter 26

Restored after Going Through the Fire!

"When you walk through the fire,
you will not be scorched,
Nor will the flame burn you."
—Isaiah 43:2

What an amazing journey! My marriage has been restored for two years. This journey started when for the second time my husband and I were attempting to get a divorce. I was fed up and was determined to continue my walk with God with or without my husband. I was convinced that the problem was only my husband and I was the "good" wife; and I was fed up with my husband's infidelity. I tried it all, but everything failed. My attempts to "save" the marriage turned into a never-ending circle. I felt trapped and finally had lost all hope. Thank the Lord that He doesn't lose hope and He is faithful! I always prayed to God about the situation, until I finally I accepted the lie that "God had someone else better for me, (a real godly man)."

One day in October our church was having a family retreat. My husband and I decided to go for our two children. Saturday night the power of the Holy Spirit moved tremendously and the Lord touched my heart to forgive my husband once again. I thought it was crazy and impossible, but I knew I had to be obedient! I fell on my knees exhausted, tired, and weak; and I prayed that I needed Jesus to strengthen me. I laid it all down to Him; what I wanted in a man, husband, and father for our children. That same night, a woman came to me and handed me her phone number. She said that she really wanted to talk to me! I called her and we met that same week. She introduced me to Restore Ministries and gave me a copy of Erin's book *How God Can and Will Restore Your Marriage*. She was praying with another sister in Christ on the phone for their marriages and I decided to join them!

I praise the Lord for Erin and her ministry. The book was a complete eye opener. The way the Lord revealed Himself to me was amazing! I cried so much when I realized my faults and errors. God is so merciful that through the pain, I was set free! I surrendered myself completely to Him. He changed me, molded me, and made me new. Through forgiveness He gave me a new love for my husband and I was blinded to any of my husband's faults. I now love, honor, and submit to my husband as to the Lord. I truly believe that what I went through was God getting my attention to trust solely in Him! When we try to fix things, the change is temporary. We need to let go and let God! Run to Him only in all things; He is the head of all men!!

Through all my changes, the battle had just begun. The hard part was about to come, but "greater is He that is in us, than he that is in the world." My faith was tested and I was determined to go THROUGH the fire, not stay in it! My husband once again was with an OW. He had never openly done so and this time he involved the children, which was very hard. He never left the home although he said he would! I took the scriptures and was obedient to the Word. God amazingly gave me the strength to see the situation as what it was: temporary, not permanent! When my husband was away, I took it as time to get closer to my Lord. I fell deeper and deeper in love with Him. He became my "everything" and nothing could take my joy away, no circumstance or situation!

It was not an easy journey! I prayed constantly, fasted, and declared scripture with God's promises. My attitudes, thoughts, and actions all reflected on God's Promises. My faith and belief did not come from what I saw, but from what God had for me. Every scripture with every word written in Erin's book became my lifestyle. I learned so much! The more I let go, the more I saw the miracles and changes. I was no longer the one trying with my flesh; I now put my trust in God's Holy Spirit. I knew the changes He made were permanent!

As the scripture says, the adulteress woman is sweet as honey, but then becomes bitter as wormwood. God's word never fails! By January, my husband broke it off with the OW. He asked for forgiveness and was amazed how I continued to love him no matter what! I think for the first time we experienced unconditional love for each other. I give all the glory to Jesus! We had a wonderful anniversary in February.

Since our restoration, I continue to keep strong in my walk with the Lord. I wouldn't have it any other way! As I trust in God for everything, my husband is our provider, spiritual leader, and a Godly man! We now have a strong marriage standing on the Rock! I have so many testimonies that I try to share as much as I can with other women who feel no hope. I must say to all of you: "GOD CAN AND WILL RESTORE YOUR MARRIAGE! NOTHING is impossible with God!"

~ *Lota RESTORED in Puerto Rico*

Ministry Note: Recently Lota felt led to write a more detailed account of her restored marriage, that we are sharing also in this book—which I am sure you will enjoy!

Looking back, the turning point began when I was attending a family retreat with my husband and children. I had already attained a lawyer for our divorce and was there for the "children." My husband had been unfaithful various times and I had had enough. At that point there was no more tears, because I deserved better. The Saturday night of the retreat my daughter, 11 at the time, went to the altar and started crying. I went up a bit after to support her. She looked at me and said "please don't leave me."

The children were unaware of the divorce, but I guess my daughter felt what was happening to our family in her spirit. I started to cry because Nina is my husband's daughter from a previous marriage, but we have raised her since she was 3. Even though I didn't give birth to her, I love her like my own. At that moment, I promised I would not leave her. I fell on my knees and cried out to God to please help me and confessed that I could not do this on my own. I cried out to Him with my heart's desires and left it at His feet. That very night I met a women who gave me the RYM book and my life has never been the same. Miraculously, the lawyer never contacted either of us again. :)

So I got the book and started reading it. I just remember praying for God to open my heart to Him. I had heard everyone else's advice, but I wanted Him to speak to me. I was in shock as the Word of God became so real and bold. I felt like the veil was removed from my eyes and I could see clearly all my faults and what God's purpose was for me. He gave me a new heart and a new love for Him. He healed me and all my hurts and the ability to see my husband with **His** eyes.

As I read the book and was ready to be the women, wife and mother God wanted me to be is when the real trials began—one of the most difficult things the Lord called me to walk through. One night my husband sat me down to talk. He told me he met someone else and it was serious, so serious that he wanted the children to meet her. (In the past he had many OWs, but never openly to allowed me or the children to know about her.)

The old me would have flipped, but God just gave me this calmness and peace so I just listened and accepted. My husband couldn't believe it and had to make sure I was listening and understood. I told him I did understand and he then left. He never physically left the house, but I let him go and never looked for him or called him.

At that point the Lord became my everything. **EVERY** tear, concern, feeling, and need I gave it to Him. I didn't speak much, only when necessary, and never ever asked questions, because it was no longer my problem but God's. The Lord sustained me and I wanted all the glory to be His. There was sooo many tests, large and small, but I always saw them as just that, tests.

Thoughout I knew God was in control and He had permitted everything for a reason. He took away the fear and replaced it with willingness to serve Him. I always submitted to His will and got through any trial He has allowed because He is worthy. I loved Him more than anything and anyone. I would need a whole other section to list all He has gotten me through. :)

In the beginning I was praying and always seeking Him. I was not used to doing this so I didn't "feel" much. I was persistent and pressed forward because He was all I had. The more I ran to Him the more I would see Him move and I truly fell in love with Him.

Then, I was praying one night, like I had been doing for quite some time and I was declaring the scriptures I had written down on cards. All of a sudden I felt this boldness come over me and the **POWER** of His word really touched me. It was like my spiritual self was no longer a baby but had become fully grown. That was when I felt His word come alive, IF GOD IS WITH ME WHO CAN BE AGAINST ME. All fear was gone and my trust was and is completely in Him. I didn't have to worry about the future or what was to come, I will always have the Lord and He is all I need and want.

There are many principles the Lord taught me, one is to **Love**. If God lives in us and He is love how can we not do the same and have compassion of others. Forgiveness is very important. God showed me all my faults and He is so merciful to forgive me, so how can I **not** do the same and forgive others? Forgiveness sets you free so God can move. Love never fails. We are His instrument to show unconditional love to others. That may be the only time they will see a glimpse of God.

For me the RYM book was the most important RMI resource since it was some time after my restoration that I ever even visited the website.

So I want to encourage you dear friend, you are where God wants you to be. You may not understand and want to run far away, but God wants you to be still. Give Him your heart and you will never be the same. Always praise God, especially when the trials get tough, because it means your blessing is close! Let God be your provider and turn to Him for **everything**.

Being restored for the past 10+ years has not been easy, but God is so faithful. So stay true to your faith and obedience to God. His word is always truth and clear. Don't complicate it with the details and circumstances of your life. OBEY His word and LOVE him more than anything and anyone. You were called with a purpose, to do not as the world does, but live completely for Him. He is worth every tear, sacrifice and humiliation. He deserves everything and more. When you choose to love, forgive and obey—the enemy will flee!

Blessings!!

~ *Lota in Puerto Rico*

Ministry Note: Lota became one of our key minisers, overseeing and expanding our Spanish Ministry. As a result she's contributed to many of our newsletters and want to include these in her Restored Marriage Testimony.

"Mothering & Healing"

"Remember, our Message is not about ourselves; we're proclaiming Jesus Christ, the Master. All we are His messengers, errand runners from Jesus for you. It started when God said, 'Light up the darkness!' and our lives filled up with light as we saw and understood God in the face of Christ, all bright and beautiful." 2 Corinthians 4:5-6 The Message (MSG)5-6

As women, we are created in a very special way with many roles to play as we walk this journey of life, (daughter, wife, mother). Now in Christ we are new creations with new roles or a new identity. We are a Spiritual daughter and bride to our Heavenly Husband. We are His and He is ours. So beautiful, as we are called the LIGHT of this dark world. So this Mother's Day, I want to celebrate as we are called to be Spiritual Mothers to those the Lord brings around us. Each of us uniquely created to serve the Lord by serving others in need with our testimony.

"So we're not giving up. How could we! Even though on the outside it often looks like things are falling apart on us, on the inside, where God is making new life, not a day goes by without his unfolding grace. These hard times are small potatoes compared to the coming good times, the lavish celebration prepared for us. There's far more here than meets the eye. The things we see now are here today, gone tomorrow. But the things we can't see now will last forever." 2 Corinthians 4:16-18 The Message

Can you believe that every moment, situation and circumstance has been perfectly created for you to be where you are at this moment for a greater purpose? Resting in the Lord as we seek Him first in all things for our ministry, our homes and for this hurting world. We know God and trust that we are always in His perfect will as we rely on Him. Let's be willing to nurture, love and have compassion for all those the Lord brings around us—just as a mother would to her own child. May we always be willing to love unconditionally without giving up no matter how things look around us because He is making us new for a grand celebration that is eternal.

2 Corinthians 5:20 The Message

"We're Christ's representatives. God uses us to persuade men and women to drop their differences and enter into God's work of making things right between them. We're speaking for Christ himself now: Become friends with God; he's already a friend with you."

When I was asked to share about someone the Lord brought into my life to mother, instantly the Lord spoke to me about a young lady named Nina. I have known her since she was very young. You see, she is my EH's daughter and at the age of 3, her biological mother, who lived out of the state, gave my EH custody. At the time we met, we were not yet married, but simply dating. When she turned 4, we got married and became a family. I would love to say we lived happily ever after, but it was a tough road. I was put in a position to step into the role of the "mother" in this child's life who felt rejected and confused as to "why" she could not be with her biological mom. I had no support from her mom and instead was very often criticized, ridiculed and mistreated, which is understandable now, but at the time, it made everything more difficult.

I tried my best to mother Nina, but being so young, only 18 years old, this new and added responsibility made me feel like a failure. Then one day something changed. This is before I even came to this ministry for my marriage. I was attending a retreat and the speaker said to write down the name of anyone that has hurt me and that I needed to forgive. A strong overwhelming feeling came that this person was Niquole's mother. I simply obeyed and with all my heart I asked the Lord to help me forgive.

Ladies, this was the first time I experienced God's power in forgiveness. It was like a huge weight was lifted from me and not only was I able to see her mom differently— with compassion— something even more special happened. I was truly able to LOVE Niquole with an intense **motherly** love. I don't know how else to explain but it was as if the LORD revealed His purpose to me as to why Niquole was in MY life and nothing else mattered. Any future insults, rejection, etc... It didn't matter, I was going to LOVE this little girl with my whole being and I was no longer alone trying to do it— the Lord was with me loving her through me.

LOVE never fails, (1 Cor. 13:8) it's so powerful, and even today, years later, we have a wonderful relationship. She has a family of her own and most importantly, she Loves the Lord. She expressed how grateful she is to have ME in her life, but I say that I am the one who is SO BLESSED to have her in mine.

I feel blessed because my HH is faithful and answers even the smallest of prayers and heart's desires. It is so beautiful to know that He wants me to go to Him for everything and place it at His feet. Then, I can simply rest that He is in control.

"...Jesus went along by the Sea of Galilee, and having gone up on the mountain, He was sitting there. And large crowds came to Him, bringing with them those who were lame, crippled, blind, mute, and many others, they laid them down at His feet; and He healed them. So the crowd marveled as they saw the mute speaking, the crippled restored, and the lame walking, and the blind seeing; and they glorified the God of Israel...." Matthew 15:29-31 (NASB)

How amazing are His miracles, what a blessing to know He want to take care of even our small requests?

"Leave No Memory Hidden"

After reading Erin's Weekly Restoration Fellowship Message, "I Should Have Known", I couldn't help but remember the day when I got the *How God Can and Will Restore Your Marriage* book in my hands and I started to read the pages. I was shocked, hurt and cried. For the first time in my whole marriage, I realized I had so much to do with the destruction of my marriage. I really felt my walls being torn down and any pride I had left of "I am a good wife" crumbled. The beauty of it all, was in my unbearable pain, it was the first glimpse of clarity in my life.

The thing is that we are very blessed and fortunate. We all go through times of being ashamed and having guilt for things we may or may not have caused. God is faithful, and He brings things up from our past, that in normal circumstance, we try to hide to never think of again. Sometimes I would ask Why Lord? Why are You asking me to bring up these horrible memories? I understand now that they are for my healing.

His desire is that there is not one area of our lives He has not healed. Let me explain. He wants us to go to Him with everything. Our past, present and future. There was a season in my life where every detail of my childhood, teens were brought up in my time with Him. Oh how I had wished I had known Him then. I made so many mistakes and been through so much. But He has given me that opportunity to give it to Him and He is faithful to tell me what He thinks of me and Heals my heart of all the pain. IT is truly amazing!!! The memory is there, but not the pain and hurt. Only the Lord can do this.

Dear friend,

Please don't leave any area or memory hidden, but openly give it to God so HE can tell you what he thinks about it and see His mighty hand heal you and set you free.

"Best Thing for Me"

I have to admit that many years ago when I started my RJ, I let go of my church in obedience to the principle of allowing my EH to become the spiritual leader of the home. I was eager to do whatever it took to be right with the Lord and show Him how much I loved Him. At first it was hard because in my mind, by not going to church, I felt that "me and my household were not serving the Lord." The more I let go, the more I pressed on to the Lord and the clearer His presence became in my life. He showed me quickly not to limit Him to four walls and He could do anything in an instant, (change hearts, open and close doors, etc.). He showed me that my first ministry was my home and I was serving Him in my obedience. As I continued to seek Him and His word, it became food and LIFE to my spirit. I knew, because of this time ALONE with Him, that I can reach out to Him and Him to me at anytime or place. How beautiful is this ladies! Really knowing that I am never alone and always cared for and loved. When we allow Him to be our Spiritual leader, He fills us, completes us and heals us in supernatural ways.

Dear Friend,

How beautiful it is to know that whenever you are in need, you can run to Lord and He will supply all your needs. Fear is not from the Lord and His word says He will never leave you nor forsake you.

Give Him the chance to show you He is sufficient and more than enough. Is He not worth our time and obedience. Is His love and provision not enough that you feel the need to run to others? Humble yourselves and open your heart. Press forward and don't look back. Let go and let God be your HH. I promise you will be standing on the Rock and never shifting sand. Your HH can love you more in a moment than all the lovers could in a lifetime. He is waiting for you!

"A Beautiful Thing"

Erin's Weekly Restoration Fellowship Message, "God Points, He Clears" is a short lesson but so important. Like Erin says that she is a "doer" I find myself wanting to get everything done and learning to rest is a bit hard. But thanks for my HH who teaches me this principle. He taught me this when in my RJ I learned to be submissive to my EH. I would have a mess around the house and I knew it was my responsibility to get done. And since I knew if I didn't get to it no one else would do it. Well as I cleaned, my EH would tell me to go and watch TV with him. In my mind I would fight that idea with all the "work" I needed to get done. But the Lord would place in my heart to listen and trust in Him. So I would stop, put everything aside, and watch TV. The beautiful thing is at some other time, that I didn't even know I had, my HH would make a way for me to get everything done and it was easy!! As my HH is the best Husband ever, I listen to Him when He tells me to rest and He takes care of everything around me.

Sometimes when I work with the ministry or things of everyday life, certain tasks may get difficult. It may not be in the work itself but may be in the amount of work. I tend to press even harder thinking it is the enemy trying to stop me from doing the work. But learning to have Him as my HH and knowing He is greater than all things, I give Him my heart so He knows I am willing to press through or rest. The Key is seeking His will!

It is so true that even in the smallest of tasks about the Lord revealing His visions. When the Lord puts in my heart His desires and I try to fulfill it in my time and with my strength it gets hard with lots of obstacles. So I stop and give it to Him, letting Him know my willingness to trust in His timing and strength. Then what tried to take me all day to do gets done in minutes.

Dear Friend,

Learning to take the Lord as your HH is a beautiful thing. It means to never be alone and always have the comfort you need. Open your heart to allow Him to work in you and be the bride He wants you to be. Allow Him to share His heart with you and He can trust that in all you do, His visions are safe with you, walking together hand in hand.

"Scripture Speaks such Truth"

After studying my RMIOU Ministry Commitments this verse, "No servant can serve two Masters, for either he will hate the one and love the other, or else he will devote to one and despise the other" Luke 16:3-4, speaks such truth! It is expressed in this lesson, the importance to not be involved in any other church or ministry, but to me it also means to not have anyone or anything else before Jesus. I have learned to SG anytime I hear or read something that I may question or feel in my spirit. We are all human so it is in the intimate relationship with our HH that ultimately I can discern what He is saying or what He wants to reveal to me. Or maybe what He is asking me to do.

This ministry has brought me such truth and peace. It has not been an easy road, but I knew and know He wants me here and to follow each principle given. Over the years I have heard many preachers, whether on the radio or at a church and many times things that have been said are contrary to what this ministry has said, but most importantly contrary to what He has called me to do after seeking Him and spending time with Him. That is why its all about having HIM to guide me, He has to be first so I am not tossed by the sea here and there.

I also saw this happen to a very dear friend who never left her church. She was always divided between what the Lord had called her to do for her restoration to Him first and her EH and what her church and pastor were teaching. She was never able to trust God but just simply went by what she would see. Her church emphasized so much on rebuking sin that she was never able to see past that and see her EH with His eyes.

I will be careful on what I read or listen to. I do occasionally go to a church when my EH asks us to go with him. This was the first christian church he went to and accepted Christ in his heart. I have let go of church and am not a part of any other ministry. I have volunteered occasionally with His Angels, a non-profit that donates shoes to an orphanage.

If you've struggled in this area, please join me in praying:

Dear Lord,

I confess that for many years my heart's desire was to be members of a church and felt this had to take place for any spiritual growth. Forgive me. You spoke to me when I wanted so much for my EH to attend a men's conference. Every year he was so close to go, then something would happen. You spoke to me clearly that You can do anything and at anytime effortlessly and a "conference" was not the answer but You are. My trust must be in You! In Your timing Lord my family is in Your hands.

Dearest Heavenly Husband,

Help me to always trust in You and to always seek You in all things. Bless me with Your spirit of discernment and revelation to see Your truth and will for me and my family. Help me to see my purpose so I can serve You through this ministry.

Dear Brides,

I know this step of letting go may be difficult because we feel that this is the only way to be spiritually fed. But when we trust in God and allow Him to spiritually feed us anywhere and at anytime, you will learn that this intimacy is the best and cannot compare to anything else.

"My Trust was and IS in Him to Provide"

When I came to a point of my life where I was broken and truly experienced Jesus and my everything, I have learned not to care on money or earthly possessions. All I need is my HH and He will supply all my needs. After being renewed and so spiritually fed in this ministry, I remember the Lord starting to speak to me about tithing. I always knew about it, but not until being fed in this ministry about it, is when my heart was open and started seeing the importance of also being obedient to this truth.

I have always felt free to give not worrying about tomorrow, but I know the Lord wanted to bring me to a new level. Last year is when I starting "doing" what I was always willing to do, but for some reason or another didn't. Giving my WHOLE tithe.

My EH and I own a business, so it started where I was giving 10% of all income to our shop. Trusting that God is the one who provides all our work and will increase our customers, and even with that I was trusting that somehow my EH wouldn't have to work such long extended hours based on His promise "He will supply for us even in our sleep." Well my HH has glorified himself in that area and I wrote a PR about that.

So later on in 2014, the Lord revealed to me that yes He supplies for our business but that I needed to tithe separately on all the income that goes to us personally. So as of now, I tithe on all the income in the business, then what ever income is used for us, personal bills and expenses, I tithe on that also. At first it was hard because it was like i was giving double, but after SG He confirmed that it needed to be right and He would "open the windows of heaven" for us.

I struggle a bit with the a certain area of my finances. Let me go back. I worked as a school teacher while my EH attended to the business. For some years, our house lived off of my income only. Before coming to RMI, I nagged so much asking my EH where was all the money he was making from the business and at some point was thinking I needed to divorce him because of his lack of financial help among other things.

From the start of my RJ I SG in many areas and my finances was one of them. Not so much the tithing at the time, but the fact that I was in charge of them. I STOPPED nagging and brought all my cares to the Lord. Again my trust was and is in Him to provide and He did miraculously.

One day, my EH came to me and said, "I know it has been a long time and I am truly grateful you have not bothered me about it, but I know my responsibility and I will start providing for this house." My heart dropped and I leaped inside for Joy...my HH had touched the heart of my EH!

Well since then it has been just like that. My marriage was restored in 2002, my son was born in 2003 and since then I have not worked but instead have helped my husband in the business.

It was a huge leap of faith, since we depended solely on my income, but my HH knew the desires of my heart to stay home with my son and after much prayer He gave me confirmation and I obeyed not looking at my circumstance. He has been providing and all through our business and my EH. I do not work outside. I have been offered many job opportunities to make extra money and it sounded good, but my faithfulness is to the Lord and He wants me to allow my EH to be the sole provider, which ultimately means I am depending solely on my HH.

So now I have prayed for the Lord to touch my EH to take the role and take care of the finances, collect the money and pay the bills, since I did not want to do anything that is rightfully my EH position, but in all occasions, it is confirmed that I am to handle them.

So here is where I struggle a bit. My EH has no idea what I do with the finances. He will occasionally tell me to pay this or save this. Even when we occasionally go to church, he will give me or tell me what to give. Let me go off for a moment to share about this:

Years earlier, When we attended church, I used to put pressure on my EH to tithe,give because I wanted to be blessed. I wanted the windows of heaven to open so I would take out the checkbook ready to give. Then one day at church, my EH said "Why should I tithe or give if you do it anyway. and since you do it with my approval or not there is no need for me to do it." From that day on I STOPPED giving in front of him or telling him to do so and I SG and repented.

Now, occasionally when we go to church I just sit quietly and the last couple of times he has given his tithes and I just thank my HH for once again touching his heart.

Sorry, so now back to what I struggle with. I tithe on the business and personal income. My EH doesn't know about this. Like I said, he doesn't ask much about the finances, just an occasional question here and there. But, although I have been tithing faithfully, I have fallen behind on bills and some are 3 months behind, but my heart wants to be faithful so I tithe before anything else. I know the Lord is in control and I am SG why this is still occurring, (not having enough for all the bills on time) but regardless, I want to give what is HIS!

So at times, my EH asks why there isn't enough for these bills and I just say, it will be taken care of. Since he doesn't ask if I am tithing I don't tell him. The Lord knows I have given this to Him and to guide me if this question ever comes up and how I would be crushed not to be able to tithe if my EH says no.

So with that said if you feel led to SG with me and share what He reveals to you.

Ministry Note: As you asked, we wanted to SG with Lota since we too are interested to know His truth more fully. What He brought to my mind was the part of your testimony that your EH has turned the finances over to you to pay, and when you asked Him before on the matter of tithing at your husband's church, your husband said, "Why should I tithe or give if you do it anyway. And since you do it with my approval or not there is no need for me to do it." It's difficult to find a balance in our marriages, and though there are things each of us would prefer our husbands do, very often we still must continue doing them until he takes them over (often during a crisis) as you probably remember from A Wise Woman. As far as tithing on both your business and personal income, Erin shared that she struggled with that same issue before, but as she shared in one of the Ministry Commitments, even though it appears we are tithing double, and the enemy tries to convince us that it's why there appears not to be enough to pay bills, that even if we were mistaken, He sees our hearts. AND we can never outgive God.

So as Erin shared, she hung onto this truth, continued to tithe "double" tithing from the ministry and then again as part of her personal income, and shared she was thrilled to discover that as result, RMI is up to being able to give about half of our the monthly income away: 10% tithe and another 30-40% offering for the ministry and

By the Word of Their Testimony

also personally, she tithes 10% to RMI and then at least another 20% offering that she said she hoped to raise and did soon after. This in no way is boasting because it's ALL Him.

Lota continued...I share about tithing and the importance of it. I pray that I can lead by example and always be faithful to my HH who deserves everything.

So pray with Lota if you struggling in the same way: "If we confess our sins, He is faithful and righteous to forgive us our sins and to cleanse us from all unrighteousness."— 1 John 1:9

Lord, I come to You humbly to ask for Your wisdom with my finances. Knowing that my EH doesn't know about my tithing, and still not having enough for all the bills to pay them on time it is tough. I know Your promise is true, so forgive me if there is something I am doing wrong whether it be in my finances or in my personal life that is hindering You from rebuking the devourer. My trust is in You and my heart's desire is to be obedient no matter what my circumstances show.

My Love,

Help to seek You more on how I handle the finances with the business and the personal income. Show me Your will and bring me Your peace that surpasses all understanding. May I seek you in everything I purchase, pay etc. That I do nothing apart from You.

Dear Brides,

Like every principle shared in this ministry that is based on the word of God, it is truth and we need to obey with no hesitation. See the Lord's faithfulness when we are faithful to Him.

~ *Lota in Puerto Rico*

Chapter 27

Confirmed Testimonies

"Your **testimonies** are fully confirmed;
Holiness befits Your house,O LORD, forevermore."
—Psalm 93:5

Here are just a MORE shorter restored marriage testimonies to encourage you!

These testimonies used to be in the *Word of Their Testimony* book, but were removed to make space for NEW and exciting "first person" (written by the person restored). These "third person" (written by someone else for the person restored) are no less MIRACULOUS and ENCOURAGING!

Most of these testimonies were the result of our first book, *How God Can and Will Restore Your Marriage*, that was published before our Fellowship, which helped launch our website. Now we are blessed to get testimonies sent to us directly from the person (primarily from our Restoration Fellowship) who is praising God for restoring their hopeless marriage!

We knew we needed to put them somewhere, but are overrun with new testimonies (what a wonderful problem to have!); that's when we decided that as long as we receive restored marriage testimonies, we will print new books. You may also notice that many have a * next to their name. This is because we never thought to ask permission to use their name. Therefore, we sometimes chose fictitious names, and sometimes kept their real name and put an * thereby protecting their identity.

With so *many* testimonies that we have posted on many different pages of our website, along with our *Word of Their Testimony* books, you would be hard pressed to find testimonies similar or the same as your situation. However, if you do fail to see a testimony just like your situation, we *know* it is because God wants to restore *your* marriage in order to encourage someone else. Therefore, it is something to REJOICE about rather than fret over.

We pray that these testimonies, along with all the others on our site and in our first *WOTT* book, will encourage and strengthen your faith to believe for *your* marriage!!

"Wife a New Woman!!"

A man contacted us from our church. He left a message on our voice mail that he was desperate for help. He said he had been counseled by his associate pastors, along with other Christian friends, to counter-sue his wife for divorce and to put a restraining order on her to protect their children! He said he and another man were on their way to where she was staying, to confront her and her lover!

When we called him back, both my husband and I got on the phone and listened as he recounted the escalating series of events of the previous few weeks. I had to ask my husband to interrupt him since I could no longer bear to hear any more details! At this point, we began to share the TRUTH with him. He was open and more than willing to embrace the Biblical principles that we shared. He kept repenting throughout the conversation for failing to deal with his wife Biblically.

It seems their trouble began after God had miraculously restored their marriage. Right after the restoration, his wife became extremely ill. He confessed to "not seeking the Lord first" but seeking many physicians. ("...he did not seek the LORD, but the physicians" 2 Chronicles 16:12). Each prescribed more and more medication for her painful condition. At the end of his rope, he sought the Lord for his wife. His prayers were answered when the doctors suddenly realized that they had *misdiagnosed* his wife. They recommended she have surgery to correct the problem, which she did.

Unfortunately, it was all part of the devil's scheme. Her pain was gone after surgery, but she found herself addicted to the pain medication she had been taking.

Again, he confessed to not seeking the Lord, but the arm of the flesh. He made the mistake of committing his own wife to a drug rehab center! In the center, she met a man, another drug addict. She then committed adultery there and was convinced that she loved this new man, not her husband. We shared that he was who put her into a place where there was no protection, and because of her vulnerability as a woman, especially with all that she had had to endure with her illness and then major surgery on top of it, he had failed as a husband.

Then both of his wife and the other man checked out of the center and moved in together. At this point, she contacted her husband to tell him that they were through as a couple, that she had met the man she loved, and that she wanted a divorce and had already filed. When her husband fought back, she told him she also wanted the children. This is when all the legal battle began and when he finally got in touch with us.

After listening to everything, we encouraged this man to first drop ALL legal action against his wife, which meant also releasing his attorney. We asked that he NOT shame his wife anymore and to simply refuse to talk to ANYONE about their situation anymore. We then told him that the next time she contacted him, he should tell her that he had released his attorney and would never take any legal action against her, ever. Then we encouraged him take full responsibility for everything. To tell her how TOTALLY and COMPLETELY this entire mess was HIS FAULT, that she was not responsible for ANYTHING, that he loved her more than ever and that if she needed ANYTHING, he would be waiting by the phone to help her.

His wife called back that very same day, and he told us that everything that we had encouraged him to do, with a heart of love for his wife and humility in his voice, she said she was shocked!! That very same day she called to say she didn't know what to do. She did want to come home, but didn't know how to do it! He told her just to drive home and he would handle the rest.

When she walked into the house, she was met with open arms and a dozen red roses!

A few minutes later her husband jumped into his car and drove to the apartment where she had been staying. He went in, packed up all of her belongings and loaded all her things and headed for home. As he drove he sang, "I took back what he (the devil) stole from me!"

A few days later, we received a phone call from his very tearful and grateful wife. She told us that she had no idea what had happened to her. She said she was completely deceived!! But when her husband told her that it was his fault and took the entire responsibility, suddenly, it's like a veil was removed from her eyes! In an instant her feelings changed completely! She said that she could NEVER repay us for saving her.

To this day we see this couple sitting in the front row of every service. Just recently, the husband read the men's book over and over again during a prolonged fast. At the end of the fast, he couldn't believe the change in his wife! He said that the Lord completely transformed her into the Godliest woman he had ever seen!!!

~ *Bob and his wife are now RESTORED in Florida*

"A Divine Appointment"

A couple of weeks after my husband and I shared our restored marriage testimony at our church, I saw a woman dragging another woman by the arm toward me. "There," she said, "you need to talk to her!"
The woman didn't share anything about her situation, but I knew just by looking at her. I just began to speak as the spirit moved me. Tears ran down her face as I spoke. When I had finished I asked if she had a restoration book and she shook her head no. When I went to my purse, I saw the *How God Can and Will Restore Your Marriage* book that I had brought for another woman that night. I told her that God had obviously wanted **her** to have it since the other woman had not shown up. Tears ran down her cheeks, onto my feet and puddled on the floor.

Then several days later, a woman came up to me and said, "You're Trish, aren't you?" Then she went on to tell me she was the lady I just told you about. She said that her husband had been in adultery for over two years and she had just come to the end of any hope when this other woman brought her to meet me. She said that she read the *How God Can and Will Restore Your Marriage* book over and over and God started to change her. She said that she didn't really DO anything, except to read the book over and over and that it was God Who had done all the changing in her.

She said that her husband had come home for a visit "unannounced and unexpectedly" and couldn't believe how different she looked, acted and most importantly reacted. The changed made him so drawn to her that he wouldn't leave. To make a long story short, she said he moved home!!!! But that's not all. She said that her husband asked if he could come to church with her and her son the next Sunday. This is the first time he had gone to church in years, and it was Father's Day (an answer to her children's prayers)! It was such a powerful and convicting sermon about being a godly man for the family unit that when our pastor asked the men who had NOT been the kind of husbands and fathers they should be to come down, her husband went to the altar to repent!! Then she said her husband has continued attending church and a couple of weeks later even volunteered to work at our 4th of July picnic!! She said this is so "unlike him"!!

She told me that although her husband is definitely through with the OW, the OW continues to call to try and get her husband back. She said that when she starts to fear, she goes back "to the book" and finds peace that "what God began HE will finish!"

Then she thanked me.

I want to thank the Lord, for He is the One Who allows me to sit in the front seat of His miracles of restoration. I am nothing and He, praise you Jesus, is EVERYTHING!!! How He could take a sinner like me, how He could take a tragedy like divorce, how He could take all of this and then allow us the privilege of using me, a vessel of wood for His good use. He is awesome and I love Him!! Thank you for convicting me to always keep one of Erin's books with me at all times, knowing You will send the brokenhearted to me!

~ *Trish in Missouri, RESTORED*

Update:

I submitted a restored marriage I was apart of that mentioned a women I had spoken to and given a book to. I wanted to share more how His Divine Appointments continue. On Sunday morning our pastor read some praise reports. The first one he read said, "A marriage restored after three years of believing and praying!"

Then, later, in the altar room a woman told me that she was the woman whom I had spoken to six months earlier. That night after prayer meeting she had stood there crying and broken. She couldn't speak except to say tearfully, "My husband has been gone for two and a half years living with someone else."

That night I shared just a bit about what God can do, and assured her that NOTHING is impossible with God. I suggested she get the *How God Can and Will Restore Your Marriage* book. Then I remembered that I had brought a book for another woman who was supposed to meet me there that night. We were standing alone, so I said, "This book must have been for you. The Lord prompted me to bring one. I thought it was for someone else, but I guess He wanted it for you all the time." Her tears dropped onto my hand and then my feet as I held the book out to her.

Six months later, Sunday night after the praise report was read, I saw her standing just a few feet away. I almost didn't recognize her — joy covered her face this time. She told me that her husband had accepted the Lord the previous Sunday and that he had been there for both services that day (hearing messages that were "perfect" for him!). She told me that she had been a part of our online Restoration Fellowship and had just gotten a new ePartner who was wonderful! Then her husband suddenly walked up. Jodie's face showed a slight panic, not knowing what I might say to him. Knowing about discretion, I simply introduced myself and told him it was nice to meet him and introduced him to my husband and my oldest son who also walked up. We all chatted a bit and then her husband said, "I guess we should go." Watching them walked off TOGETHER, she turned and looked over her shoulder, her face beaming.

GOD IS SO GOOD!!! He had two divine appointment six months apart — when we first met and then the second one to let me see His amazing work standing in front of me. Thank you Lord, You're divine appointments never cease to amaze me!!

~ *Jodie RESTORED in Missouri*

In Conclusion

There are MANY more testimonies that are posted on our website! Recently we've published at lease ONE NEW testimonies each week that we are now getting into a new *Word of Their Testimony* book— creating a series of hope.

What you have read is only a very *small sample* of the POWER and FAITHFULNESS of God that are told through countless restored marriages!

Don't let ANYONE try to convince you that God cannot restore YOUR marriage! It is a lie. The TRUTH is that He is MORE THAN ABLE!!

Is Your Marriage... Crumbling? Hopeless? Or Ended in Divorce?

At Last There's Hope!

Have you been searching for marriage help online? It's not by chance, nor is it by coincidence, that you have this book in your hands. God is leading you to Restore Ministries that began by helping hundreds of marriages that *appear* hopeless—like yours—and has done the impossible by restoring them.

God has heard your cry for help in your marriage struggles and defeats. He predestined this **Divine Appointment** to give you the hope that you so desperately need right now!

We know and understand what you are going through since many of us in now have a restored marriage and family! No matter what others have told you, your marriage is not hopeless! We know, after filling almost books of restored marriage testimonies, that God is able to restore any marriage—especially yours!

"Behold, I am the LORD, the God of all flesh; is anything too difficult for Me?" (Jeremiah 32:27).

If you have been told that your marriage is hopeless or that without your spouse's help your marriage cannot be restored, don't believe it! Each week we announce a new Restored Marrriage from someone—why not yours?!

"Ah Lord GOD! Behold, You have made the heavens and the earth by Your great power and by Your outstretched arm! Nothing is too difficult for You"! (Jeremiah 32:17).

If you have been crying out to God for more help, someone who understands, then we invite you to join our Restoration Fellowship. Since beginning this fellowship, we have seen more marriages restored on a regular basis than we ever thought possible!

Restoration Fellowship

Restoration is a "narrow road"—look around, most marriages end in divorce! But if your desire is for a restored marriage, then our Restoration Fellowship is designed especially for you!

Since beginning this fellowship, we have seen marriages restored more consistently than we ever thought possible.

Let us help you stay committed to "working with God" to restore your marriages by helping you find your heavenly Husband—a Husband who will heal your hurts and once healed, restore your marriage. Restoration Fellowship can offer you the help, guidance, and support you will need to stay on the path that leads to victory—*your* marriage restored and healing!

Let us assure you that all of our marriages were restored by GOD (through His Word) as we each sought Him to lead us, teach us, guide us and transform us through His Love. This, too, is all *you* need for *your* marriage to be restored.

However, God continues to lead people to our ministry and fellowship to gain the faith, support and help that so many say that they needed in their time of crisis.

I really do want to thank you for providing my first stepping stone for a restored life. This is the start of my journey and I want you know I will work as hard as I can to finish the race and help others to follow in Gods word. I want you to understand it is not just a resorted marriage I am looking for, it is having a restored Life that I need.

There is not any thing better than knowing you have saved someones life and believe me when I say everyone at RMI has helped save my life. I am not just saying that either. From the bottom of my heart thank you for helping me on my journey to find my life!

To start I would recommend Erin's book "How God Can and Will Restore Your Marriage" to anyone who is truly wants to restore their marriage, because they first need to find God and discover His word. It is a difficult path to walk but that's why I would recommend this book to anyone that really wants to walk it.

Ohh Ladies, my marriage is like so many others out there. I know from the day my husband told me that he was leaving it was from God. I knew He was telling me that I need to change. My husband was forever telling me how much he loved me and would call me just to play a song he heard on the radio, or while it was playing, to tell me it reminded him of me. This was happening right up to December. Then in a strange twist of fate he told me on Christmas day he was leaving and was going to date his Boss. He dated her for oh about a week then moved into her house with her. I know that God has called me to change and to look at myself. My husband is not the issue, now I know that I am. Do not get me wrong, he has plenty to answer to but not to me to God alone.

Lord, I just want to thank you for allowing me to get into this mess so I could find You through this ministry. I am thanking You in advance for helping me get through this and to understand why I need to get there—to really find You. I do not really see an answer yet but I know you are faithful and will provide for me.

Thank you dear fellowhsip members for sticking by me.

Join our Restoration Fellowship TODAY and allow us to help YOU **restore** YOUR marriage—and find your Heavenly Husband.

Restore Ministries International

POB 830
Ozark, MO 65721
USA

For more help
Please visit one of our Websites:

EncouragingWomen.org

HopeAtLast.com

RestoreMinistries.net

RMIEW.com

AjudaMatrimonial.com (Portuguese)

AyudaMatrimonial.com (Spanish)

Zachranamanzelstva.com (Slovakian)

EncouragingMen.org

Made in the USA
Middletown, DE
28 February 2023

25828906R00119